While many people are likely familiar with psychic mediums who do readings, few know about healing mediums, who teach you how to clear illnesses and ailments in a noninvasive, peaceful way. Anysia Marcell Kiel guides you on a journey to awaken powerful healing abilities within yourself through her remarkable life stories and client sessions. Learn about clearing karmic imprints, communicating with loved ones in spirit, integrating the soul path, and much more. You have the ability to heal yourself, and although you may not remember how yet, Anysia's experiences and insights will show you how to embrace love, live your life purpose, and align with your soul.

Discovering
the
Healer
Within

About the Author

Anysia Marcell Kiel, MFA, is a healing medium who has been able to communicate with spirits since she was a child. She is the author of *Discovering the Medium Within: Techniques and Stories from a Professional Psychic Medium,* which received the following literary accolades: 2013 USA Best Book Award, 2013 Living Now Gold Medal Book Award, 2014 New England Book Festival Award, and 2015 Indie Spiritual Book Award.

Anysia holds an MFA in creative writing and enjoys sharing information and exercises via her blog, written for those who are interested in learning more about mediumship development and healing.

Anysia is the founder of the Soul-Centered Healing Method, a system of healing that incorporates divine energy. This healing method identifies and clears the root causes and imprints of illnesses, disease, trauma, and repetitive life patterns. Anysia created Soul-Centered Healing LLC, a spiritual healing center in Toms River, NJ, through which she provides healing sessions, classes, lectures, and events. Anysia lives in New Jersey with her two children, Brayden and Briella, who have the same abilities as their mother. To learn more about Anysia and to access her blog, visit her website at www.anysiakiel.com.

AUTHOR OF *DISCOVERING THE MEDIUM WITHIN*

ANYSIA MARCELL KIEL

Discovering
the
Healer
Within

USE CHAKRAS & INTUITION TO CLEAR NEGATIVITY & RELEASE PAIN

Llewellyn Publications
WOODBURY, MINNESOTA

FIRST EDITION
First Printing, 2017

Book design by Rebecca Zins
Cover design by Lisa Novak

Llewellyn Publications is a registered trademark
of Llewellyn Worldwide Ltd.

The Library of Congress Cataloging-in-Publication Data
Names: Kiel, Anysia, author.
Title: Discovering the healer within : use chakras & intuition to clear
    negativity & release pain / Anysia Marcell Kiel.
Description: First edition. | Woodbury, Minnesota : Llewellyn
    Publications, [2017]
Identifiers: LCCN 2017027385 (print) | LCCN 2017014167 (ebook)
    | ISBN 9780738752877 (ebook) | ISBN 9780738752471 (alk. paper)
Subjects: LCSH: Healing—Miscellanea. | Occultism. | Spiritual healing.
    | Mental healing.
Classification: LCC BF1439 (print) | LCC BF1439 .K47 2017 (ebook)
    | DDC 615.8/528—dc23
LC record available at https://lccn.loc.gov/2017027385

Llewellyn Publications
A Division of Llewellyn Worldwide Ltd.
2143 Wooddale Drive
Woodbury, MN 55125-2989
www.llewellyn.com

Printed in the United States of America

For Brayden and Briella.

I wouldn't be who I am in this life

if your souls hadn't chosen me as your mother.

Thank you for teaching me how to give and receive

unconditional love; it is the greatest gift.

May you shine your lights brightly and

make this world a better place.

Namaste, and all my love to both of you always,

Mom

Acknowledgments

I would like to thank my amazing editor, Amy Glaser, for her insight and publishing acumen. I am grateful to have had the pleasure of working with her for my first and second books. She is a consummate professional and a trustworthy mentor. Thank you to my production editor, Becky Zins, for her timely efforts in monitoring content consistency and viewing the book from the reader perspective. She was a pleasure to work with on this book.

Contents

Introduction

Everyone comes to earth with the ability to heal themselves, but they don't always remember how to do it. For most of us it's a process that unfolds like a beautiful flower unfurling itself one soft petal at a time. Sometimes it's painful and difficult, but the more we clear and heal, the more we allow the soul to come through and the more we shine.

My journey of remembering and helping others awaken was documented in my first book, *Discovering the Medium Within: Techniques & Stories from a Professional Psychic Medium*. I eventually accepted all my abilities as a healing medium, but a catalyst for my recall was having two children with the same abilities as me. These two beautiful souls gifted from the universe really helped me to remember who I am and why I came to this earth. My abilities are an integral part of me now, and I use them daily in my work with clients. We journey together in sessions to clear karmic imprints and align them with the soul path. It's a beautiful process, and I'm grateful to be part of the healing experience of others.

If we take a step back from situations that scar us and remove the emotions, we will find that those experiences were shared with love all for our highest good. Perhaps someone had an undernurturing mother or experienced rejection from a parent. What did that soul learn from that experience? Maybe the soul learned to be strong and independent. Maybe that soul needed to learn that lesson early on in life so they could be prepared for the intense work they would do as an adult. If we look at things through the soul's eyes, on a soul level rather than an emotional one, we will see what the experience is really about. Those who challenge us the most in this life have the greatest gifts to give us and help us grow the most.

In this life we are here to live our soul purpose and experience love. Before we can fully embrace love from anyone, we need to fully love and accept ourselves unconditionally. When we do this we heal our hearts and souls, and we live the life we are meant to live. We are all able to heal ourselves; we just need to wake up and understand what is in our way.

1

Embracing My Healing Path

For the majority of my life, I wondered why I could see, feel, and hear what other people couldn't perceive. Things that went bump in the night always had a face—sometimes a familiar one, but most times it was a complete stranger who spoke a silent language. I could discern and translate those muted words for others who couldn't hear them. My saving grace was when message recipients verified the details I relayed to them.

Due to my rigid Catholic upbringing, which didn't support psychic awareness or communication with spirits, and an immediate family that really didn't know how to handle my abilities, I tried to block out my mediumship skills so I could be "normal" like everyone else. But when I had my son, Brayden, he was able to see, feel, and hear all the things that were intangible to most people. He was only three years old when I first realized that fact. Standing in my bedroom one morning, he pointed at my bathroom doorway and casually said, "I see kids." I saw them too, standing there, quietly glaring at us. I asked him to describe what they looked like, and he relayed in detail everything I saw in front of me: the little toddler boy in a green top and brown shorts holding hands with the same-aged little girl dressed in a white cotton sundress. A sense of peace grounded me as I realized God had sent me this special soul for a reason. That peaceful grounding was rooted deeper with the birth of my daughter, Briella, who also had the same abilities. I didn't want them to grow up the way I did, feeling like a winged butterfly grounded by caterpillars. From that day forward, I accepted and embraced my abilities. In doing so, I hoped that when Brayden and Briella grew up, they wouldn't hide their wings but instead would be comfortable spreading them to soar wherever life led them.

As I worked with my abilities, I knew I didn't want to do readings for people because it just didn't seem like a fit, but I didn't know what the Divine had in store for me. I was unsure why he had made my son and me this way, but it was more than coincidence. I never took any psychic development or mediumship classes because I was born with my abilities activated. Anything I learned about my abilities was relayed from those in spirit, including my maternal grandmother, Nanny. I shared with Brayden whatever I learned about spirits, energy, and psychic awareness.

One night, while watching television, the palms of my hands mysteriously generated heat. I rubbed them together, and the temperature amplified. I had the sensation of a spinning invisible disc in the center of each hand. I placed my hands on the center of my chest. Within a few minutes, the heated sensation disseminated throughout my body, blanketing me in peace. A few days later I mentioned the experience to one of my cousins. She said that my hand chakras had opened and that it was common for natural healers to have their hand chakras open up on their own.

An older cousin of mine was teaching a level 1 Reiki class, so I signed up to study with her. On my father's side of the family there are now fifteen Reiki Masters, including both of my children. Many of my cousins are clairsentient and clairvoyant, as well. Although they are accepting of the clairsentience and clairvoyance, I only know of the clairaudience and mediumship being accepted by me, one of my siblings, and my two children, but who knows what the future generations of family members hold in the line. I have found that once one generation is accepting of abilities, the next generation is more open because they learn from the elders. When we get together for family affairs there's quite a bit of energy funneling around. I enjoyed studying with my cousin because she was a good teacher. She guided me with a deep sense of compassion. She told me that the Reiki attunements were just a formality and that I was a natural healer. I was grateful for her support as I ventured into the exciting world of healing. The more I learned, the more familiar it felt, like I was remembering something I had always known in my core being.

At first I only worked on family members. When I worked in sessions, I wasn't using the Reiki modality. I didn't place my hands on the client's body at all. I worked about six inches above the physical body. I didn't use the Reiki hand positions or symbols. Instead, I just worked intuitively, psychically scanning where I needed to go. I placed my hands over the section of the person's body and read the energy and experiences imprinted there. Then, with the client's permission, I released all the imprints. My healing method was different. We were peeling away and healing all the emotions, ideas, and experiences that were blocking the soul's path. We were aligning the person with the soul, hence the name Soul-Centered Healing. I was given the name and the method by my spirit guides to help people heal beyond physical manifestations—to help them identify why they were manifesting illnesses, so they could clear them and align with their soul paths. I knew it was different but never fully acknowledged it until one of my friends from high school came for a session.

I had known Heather since my freshman year in high school. We always kept in touch and met up a few times every year for lunch. She had made an appointment for a healing session, and I got her in right away. When she first came to the office, we sat at the white wicker table and caught up on our lives, talking about our children, our work, and of course updates on other friends from high school. It was her first time in the new office, and Heather said that she loved the decor with angels and plants, which gave it a garden feel.

"I love the energy in this place; it's so peaceful," she noted.

"The plants and natural light keep the vibes high, and I have clear quartz crystal grids on the floor and along the ceiling. The crystals are self-cleansing and they keep the energy balanced," I said. She looked around the room as I pointed out all the crystals in the square-shaped grids.

"It definitely makes a difference. I can feel it," Heather said with a smile. When she smiled she dipped her face slightly into her chest, and all I could see was the crown of her short brown hair. I knew something was bothering her but figured it would come up in the session, so I didn't mention it. We made our way over to the massage table and she reclined comfortably as I pulled the white sheet and soft matching blanket up from her feet to her chest. I said an opening prayer to center and shield the space, and we began the session. I moved my hands about six inches above her body and scanned her energetic field. The aura held jagged gray energy that felt heavy and chaotic.

"Wow, somebody's got a lot going on, being pulled in a bunch of different directions," I commented.

"Exactly. It's been crazy," Heather said. After I cleared and balanced her aura, my hand was drawn to the sacral chakra, right below her belly button. On a physical level, the sacral chakra is the center for sexual energy and governs the ovaries and uterus in women. It also houses the psychic sense of clairsentience, which means "clear feeling." This sense allows us to perceive energy through feeling. We can ascertain the energy of other people, as well as environmental energy. As I scanned her sacral chakra, I could see it was misshapen and not spinning properly. I could feel that her hormones were a bit out of balance and knew that she was experiencing mood swings. I placed my hands directly over Heather's sacral chakra to see what was stored in there. As though I were viewing a video from her childhood, I saw and felt a memory that was imprinted there. She was sitting alone on a couch waiting for her mother to play with her, but her mother was hurrying around the house doing other things. I heard her ask her mother to play with her, but her mother said that she was too busy. I could feel Heather's sadness associated with the memory; it was stored in the emotional layer of the aura. I knew from what I had seen that Heather had been a sensitive child who needed nurturing and attention but didn't get much of it from her mother early on.

I told her what I saw, and she confirmed the experience and also noted that it happened all the time; her mother was always busy doing other things. I asked Heather if she was ready to let all of that go, and she said that she wanted to release it. We pulled these imprints out, cleared them through all the auric layers, and then filled the areas with white light to balance them. I explained to Heather that when we had unfavorable imprints stored in an area of our bodies, we could manifest ailments or illnesses there to let us know that something in that place needed to be addressed and healed. She listened quietly.

Next, I moved my hands to her throat chakra, located in the center of her throat. The throat chakra governs the physical throat, sinuses, ears, and thyroid. It is our energy center for speaking up for ourselves and voicing our truth. On a metaphysical level it houses three of our psychic senses, which is why I call it the psychic powerhouse. The senses located there are clairaudience, clairscent, and clairgustance. Clairaudience means clear hearing; we use this sense to communicate telepathically. Clairscent, also known as clairalience, is the ability to smell clearly; using this sense, we can smell things from spirit—things not physically present. Clairgustance means clear tasting and allows us to taste things that are not physically present. Perhaps someone's grandmother was a coffee drinker and when she visits in spirit, her grandson tastes coffee, though he is not drinking it. As I held my hand over the area, the chakra was the size of a golf ball rather than its normal size, which is like a baseball or the size of an adult palm in the center of the hand. The energy was slow there, like honey, and I could see there were issues with her mom that needed to be communicated but instead were trapped in that energy center.

"What's the deal with your mom and these things you need to say to her that you're holding in to avoid conflict?" I questioned. Heather raised her eyebrows and I smiled calmly. "No reindeer games here, Rudolph. We dig in and get our hands dirty in this office," I said. She chuckled.

"Uh, yeah—no shit. I get that!" she said. "My mom's very stubborn. Everything has to be her way. She never listens to me, so I never tell her anything," she explained. I told Heather that she needed to get those things out and communicate them, even if she wrote them out on paper and threw it away or just said them out loud to herself. The energy was backed up, and she could have some throat-related issues if she didn't start releasing some of the energy there. She said she would work on it.

A few seconds later an elderly woman came into view by the right side of the massage table. She had a kind face with a huge smile, and I could feel her emitting warm, loving energy. She said she was Heather's maternal grandmother. As soon as I told Heather her grandmother was present, tears slipped down her cheeks like raindrops before a storm and she said her name, "Muzzy," in a soft whisper. Her grandmother had recently passed, and Heather said she had hoped Muzzy would visit during the session. Her grandmother said she had connected to Heather in a dream visit right after her passing. In the dream she asked Heather to go out to breakfast, which had been one of her favorite things to do when she was on earth. Heather confirmed what Muzzy was saying. I could tell by the things Muzzy was saying that this woman was very nurturing and motherly to Heather.

She instructed Heather to exercise patience and acceptance in dealing with her mother because she had a difficult personality.

Muzzy said that Heather's mother was always a little demanding as a child, and that personality trait developed further in her adulthood. Heather listened attentively while tears slid down her cheeks. Muzzy explained that Heather's mom was not trying to ostracize her or overlook her needs; she was just very concerned with her own self rather than the needs of others. Muzzy said that was why God sent her to Heather. Even though Heather didn't have a deep connection with her own mother, her connection to her maternal grandmother was deep and loving, filling the maternal cavity in her life. Muzzy treated Heather like she was her own daughter. They did everything together, and Heather could confide in her. Before Muzzy left the session, she told Heather that she would come to her in dreams and if Heather needed help with anything, she just had to ask, either aloud or silently in her thoughts.

I finished balancing Heather's energy, and then I said the final prayer of gratitude to end the session, cut energetic cords, and remove any residual energy. When Heather rose from the table, I placed my hands on her shoulders, pulled all her energy from her head down to her feet, and grounded her deeply. Then I guided her over to the cushioned loveseat so her energy could continue to settle. She sat across from me as I stripped the sheets and blankets off the massage table. Her eyes looked a little glazed over, and she seemed tired, with her shoulders slumped forward. A lot of information had been conveyed that would take some time to mentally process. I told her that she would experience a physical clearing of the energetic imprints over the next week. I explained that although it was energy work, it still had to clear out of the physical body.

"You may feel a little emotional because we opened and balanced your sacral chakra. If you find yourself crying when you're watching a comedy, just allow it to happen." Heather laughed. "I'm serious. Plus you might have a little bit of digestive upset because we cleared some very old fears out of the root chakra."

"That's awesome. I can't wait until that happens tomorrow at work," she said. I also told her the throat chakra was shifting open and she would be clearing her throat over the next few days, just as she had during the session. She listened to what I said and then asked me a pretty direct question.

"So what is this really that you do here? I've had Reiki before, and this is nothing like it. You can see and talk to spirits in the exact tone of the person in spirit," she said, holding up one finger. "You can clearly view and hear things that happened to me from my past," she said, adding another finger, "and you know things going on currently in my life without me telling you about them," she noted, holding up a third finger. I pulled one of the wicker chairs away from the table and sat down on it directly across from her.

"Well, you know I'm a medium, obviously. I relay the information from spirit exactly as I hear it, including the specific words, details, and inflection, because everything holds meaning for the person on the table."

"Exactly. You sounded just like her, and you said specific things that she always said."

"It's kind of like everyone has this invisible book of their energy, and in it is all their imprinted experiences. I can read the book; I can see, hear, and feel everything stored in it. So when they come to me, we open the book and we go through the pages together. We take out the ones that don't serve them and replace those pages with new energy, and then we rebalance their entire energy field so they can live in line with their soul path. Plus, whoever is connected to them in spirit visits during the session and helps them heal as well."

"I think it's totally cool," she said, reaching her arms into her coat.

I told her to text me if she had any questions about the energy clearing over the next few days. She gave me a thumbs up as she left. I felt a sense of peace and gratitude for being able to help Heather heal herself.

EXERCISE
Releasing the Past

The past can hold you hostage and prisoner to old ideas and experiences. We need to let go of the past so we can be "free" in the present. It's not an easy task. In life we accumulate energetic imprints from our past that affect our vibration. These imprints are in our energetic field and when someone triggers them, we may respond negatively to avoid similar experiences. For example, a person may have been in a loving relationship with someone that violated his trust. As a result, he may have trust issues because he carries the imprints from the experience. He may push people away to avoid trusting them and perhaps being hurt. In order for him to be in a relationship where the imprints are triggered and he doesn't project his past into the current relationship, he has to heal and release those old imprints. We have to do a lot of work on ourselves, including missing out on opportunities and relationships, to get through this lesson. But if those opportunities and relationships are meant to be in our lives, they'll present themselves again when the timing is right.

Setting the past free and letting go of the imprints has been one of my biggest lessons in all aspects of life. For me, writing has always been a way to take a closer, more introspective look at things. Writing about releasing the past has helped me to dissect the process a bit deeper so I could truly understand it on a soul level.

Sometimes when people come into our lives we may not be prepared for those relationships. Those people have lessons and experiences to share with us. We might not be ready to fully process the gifts they present to us, so we throw all types of fears and projections at them, essentially showing them our shadow selves rather than the Divine within us. We might push them away and sabotage the threads of connection we've built. When they're gone, then we have an opportunity to step back from all the emotion and see why it failed.

Many of us wrap ourselves in guilt and grief over these types of situations. But if we do that, we hold ourselves in that unevolved place in the shadows, vibrating at a low rate. If we do the work and resolve the roots of our projections and fears, we may be able to repair those relationships down the road. If those relationships are meant to be part of our lives, they'll return to us again in divine timing, when all parties are on the same page, vibrating at a similar rate, and the past issues have been cleared. Forgiveness of oneself is the most important part of this process. When we forgive ourselves for any mistakes, we free our souls and open to the experience of forgiveness with others.

In my work I see so many people who stop their lives once someone close to them dies a physical death. It's as if they play a record each day that skips on the same spot, and they just cannot get past missing the physical connection. But if they heal themselves and release the past, they will find their loved ones waiting on the other side for them. Their loved ones are there to continue a new kind of relationship with them—a spiritual one based on signs, symbols, and telepathic communication. In order to get to this point, the person on the earth plane needs to let go of the past and any fears so they can raise their vibration and engage with their loved one in spirit.

One of the many choices we have in our lives is to live in the past—full of fear and regret, with words like *could have, should have*, and *would have*—or let go of all of that and accept the past for what it is: a learning tool and the vehicle that got us to the present. The past belongs in the past; it doesn't belong in the present. Reflect on it briefly, learn from it, and release it! When we forgive ourselves and others for the past, we free our souls to be fully present so we can fly with open wings through life in love, compassion, and peace.

> *What you will need for this exercise:* a piece of paper and a pen or pencil
>
> • • • •
>
> Make a list of all the experiences from your past that surface in your present life. They can be from the recent past or they can be from your childhood. These can be things that come up in your thoughts, dreams, or experiences with other people.

Next, write down everyone involved in each experience on your list. For example, maybe the first experience on your list involves a parent. You would write the experience and then the name of the parent next to it.

Go through each experience, one at a time. Think about the experience and write down the emotions you feel when you think of it. Now your list should have three things written on it:

- all the experiences from your past that surface in your present life
- the names of the people involved in each experience
- the emotions you feel when you think of each separate experience (maybe one experience elicits anger and another one raises sadness)

Consciously choose to forgive yourself and all those involved in each experience. Say it aloud.

For each experience, also say aloud that you release all imprints, cords, and associated energy. Pull everything out by the root and send it to the light.

Next, send everyone involved love, light, and healing. Send yourself loving thoughts for your own healing. Choose to love yourself unconditionally and know that all experiences in this life are for your highest good.

2

Clearing Acute Illness

When I found out I was pregnant with my daughter, I was nervous. Having had two prior miscarriages, both at the end of the first trimester, I just wanted to get through the first term without any issues. It had been a year since the last miscarriage, and I had done a great deal of healing on myself between that time and conceiving again. I hoped to deliver a healthy baby this time.

Brayden, my son, was five years old and excited about having a sibling; he said that he hoped particularly for a boy and set aside a group of Matchbox cars for his new baby brother. He asked if his new brother would have dark brown hair and hazel eyes like him. I said that I didn't know, but anything was possible. He smiled, indenting the dimple in his left cheek, as his warm golden-brown eyes grew to the size of chestnuts. I didn't bother to tell him that I knew from a premonition that I was having a girl and saw that she would have black hair like me. Early on I felt the baby was a girl, just as I knew Brayden would be a boy. In a dream one night I saw me holding her, and she was a little cutie bundled in pink with hair as dark as night. The level II ultrasound at twenty weeks officially confirmed the baby's female gender. Brayden was a little disappointed, but seeing the baby move on the ultrasound screen made it real for him, and he was excited to meet her. After the ultrasound we immediately drove to the store and bought her a pink pair of crochet booties—her first gift. Then we went to lunch to celebrate the good news.

I already knew her name. I had decided when I was in college that if I had a girl, I would name her Briella. At that time I had gone to a theater in downtown Baltimore to see *The Servant of Two Masters,* an Italian comedy written in 1743 by Carlo Goldoni. An innkeeper in the play was named Brighella. I loved the name but not the hard "g" sound. Fifteen years later I was pregnant with baby Briella. There was so much preparation for a new baby girl. I had saved all Brayden's toys and clothes, which were of no use now. My sister-in-law was also pregnant at the same time and was due two weeks before me with a little boy, so I packed Brayden's baby items and gave them to her.

After the ultrasound we decided to tell our families the gender, but we kept the name a secret; we thought it would be a nice surprise after she was born. Everyone was excited and the gender really didn't matter as long as the baby was healthy. I moved through my second trimester quickly and prepared everything for baby Briella. Brayden went shopping with me weekly and we picked out all kinds of pink outfits, matching booties, and soft blankets. At night I would rub cocoa butter on my belly and talk to my baby girl in a very soft voice. "Briella, Mommy loves you so much." Sometimes I placed my palm on my stomach and gave her energy, too. She turned and kicked inside me. I knew she'd be headstrong and independent, just like me. Motherhood was a lesson in accepting and giving unconditional love, and I looked forward to growing in that experience with baby Briella.

Brayden turned six a few weeks before Briella was born. We had a big birthday party for him at the ice skating rink and invited his whole first grade class. He was good on skates because he played hockey and could zip around on the ice like a mini NHL pro. But very few of his classmates were experienced on ice skates, so his dad and my brother-in-law were busy taking turns around the rink with the tentacles of first graders attached to them. In retrospect, it probably wasn't the best party to have for such small children, but Brayden had a blast—from the skating right down to the SpongeBob cake and cupcakes I had baked for him. I wanted the party to be a big deal so he knew he was still important, even though there was emphasis on the new baby.

Eight days before my scheduled delivery, I noticed something strange with Brayden. I walked into the downstairs bathroom after he forgot to flush the toilet, which in this case was a good thing. A red hue colored the toilet water, and I knew there was blood in it. My heart beat rapidly as I dialed his pediatrician, who said to bring Brayden in immediately. Since his office was less than two miles from our house, I put Brayden's coat on him and sped him to the doctor.

The small-framed, dark-haired doctor came into the room in his white lab coat, a clipboard under his arm and a stethoscope in his hand. He looked in Brayden's throat and said that it was a little red. He gave a him a streptococcus (strep) test, although he wouldn't know the results until the following morning, and also had Brayden give a urine sample. He then tested it with a strip and confirmed blood in the urine. The doctor's usual friendly demeanor, expressed in his big smile and upbeat tone, was transformed into something different now. He frowned and his tone deepened. He admitted that the issue fell out of his level of expertise as a pediatrician, but he said he would call Children's Hospital of Philadelphia (CHOP), the closest facility to treat pediatric kidney issues. I heard the words *pediatric kidney issues* and chills raced up my spine like an icy wind. He called and got us an appointment within two days. The doctor said he would call in the morning with the strep results and would also call in an antibiotic prescription if the results were positive. The next morning at 9:00 a.m., the doctor said that the strep test was positive and we could pick up the amoxicillin prescription at the pharmacy. He wished us good luck at the hospital and asked us to keep him in the loop.

Brayden's father didn't want me to make the drive to Philadelphia because it was a long car ride and only four days before my scheduled due date, and I agreed. He took Brayden for the initial consultation at the nephrology department at CHOP while I waited nervously at home, cleaning the house in my nesting frenzy. When they got there the doctor did a urinalysis, not only for blood in the urine but also to test if the kidneys were releasing protein. The test confirmed blood as well as high levels of protein in the urine. Based on the tests, the doctor suspected IgA nephropathy, an autoimmune disease that affects the kidneys.

According to the doctor, IgA is a protein called an antibody that the body produces in response to infection. It is supposed to get routed to the mucus membrane and tell the body to create mucus. In the disease, the IgA antibodies get misrouted into the kidneys and cause inflammation, hence the blood in the urine. The doctor said that Brayden was a little young for the illness, as he had just turned six, but the illness occasionally had been seen in young children. He said they would keep an eye on the issue. Without any real history of Brayden and this illness or other family members with the illness, it was hard to determine a prognosis. The doctor said to contact him if there was blood in the urine again.

We sent Brayden back to school and tried not to alarm him about the kidney issue he had manifested seemingly overnight. My emotions were already elevated from being pregnant, so this situation made me hypersensitive and I had to block it out of my mind to avoid anxiety. Over the next few days, I bought Brayden small gifts like puzzles and games and wrapped them up to ease the transition from being an only child for six years to having to share the spotlight with a new baby sister. I planned on giving him a new item to open each day when he visited us in the hospital.

I delivered my little dark-haired princess a few days later. When I held her in my arms for the first time, I looked into her eyes and felt love fill every cell in my body. It overwhelmed me and I could not physically contain the emotion. She was pure love and I knew this tiny soul would teach me many things in this life. Her beautiful porcelain skin contrasted sharply against her jet-black hair. Though I was physically meeting her for the first time, I felt like we had always known each other—like I found someone that I had lost long ago.

Brayden was in the waiting room and came in right away. He sat in the wooden rocking chair and held his baby sister. After a few minutes he handed her back to me and asked if he could put together the new animal puzzle he had just opened. He seemed interested in Briella but not overly excited. I anticipated there would be a ramp-up time for his adjustment.

I had my OB/GYN release me from the hospital after two days, though the insurance covered my stay for five days. The energy of the hospital was chaotic, and I felt I would rest and recover much better in the comfort of my own home. Briella adapted to her new home quickly, sleeping through the night after the first few days. She didn't cry often, but whenever she did Brayden would place his hands over his ears and ask, "Can't we send her back to the hospital? She cries too much." I explained that she was here to stay and crying was her way to let us know she needed something, since she was too little to talk. I knew she would take some getting used to for him. I tried regularly to give him big brother tasks of getting me the diapers at changing time or handing me her bottles to shift his mindset into the role of special helper. He had a brief interest in it and then went back to playing with his toys.

A few weeks after Briella came home, Brayden had blood in his urine again one morning. Since the last incident, I had gotten in the habit of checking his urine daily, and he wasn't allowed to flush it until I checked. We had it down to a routine. Every time he went to the bathroom, he called me, I checked it, and then he flushed. When I saw the red-tinted water, I contacted CHOP and they gave us an appointment the following day.

We packed the family in the car the following morning and drove out to Philly; Briella was just short of four weeks old and slept the whole car ride, while Brayden played his handheld video game. I looked out the window, saying very little, trying to hide my sadness and fears that entangled like vines in my chest. As we parked the car in the parking garage at CHOP, an overwhelming sense of dread hit me like a brick wall. It felt like all the air had been sucked out of the space by a giant vacuum, and I found myself gasping deeply to fill my lungs. As we waited for the elevator to take us from the parking garage to the main floor of the hospital, I read the list of specialized departments, many of which I'd never heard of before. I held Brayden's little hand in mine, silently saying a prayer for his healing.

The halls were a painted mural of parents and sick children brushing by us. I couldn't believe my eyes. Toddlers in hospital gowns, hairless middle-schoolers sitting in chairs with tubes of chemotherapy medications attached to them. It was all too much at once and I felt my eyes well with unshed tears. As a mother, the sight of so many sick children pierced my heart, which bled maternal love for every child there. I just wanted to get into the nephrology office so I could calm down a bit and get centered. We entered the beige office and I quickly nursed Briella. The nurses loved her because she was so tiny and sweet. Brayden played with the wooden blocks in the play area and I tried to ground my energy down to my feet.

As soon as the nurse led us to an exam room, they gave Brayden a strep test, as well as a urinalysis. The strep came back positive once again, and this time the urinalysis was a higher protein rate than it had been a few weeks prior. The doctor came in the room. His six foot four stature and medium build were an interesting contrast against his gentle personality and warm, expressive face; he was literally a gentle giant. He had a way with children and conveyed compassion and understanding in his dialogue with Brayden. I liked him immediately and knew I could trust him with Brayden's care.

He carefully explained for me (as he had done for Brayden's father during the first office visit) how IgA nephropathy was triggered by strep and how antibodies were misrouted to the kidneys and would cause irritation and hence blood and sometimes protein in the urine. I listened intently. He said that in order to truly diagnose the suspected illness, we would need to do a kidney biopsy and they would test to see if the antibodies were present in the kidneys. I immediately felt the tiny hairs on my neck raise at the sound of the word *biopsy*. I said that I wanted to hold off and if it happened a third time, then we would do it. A biopsy meant sticking a large needle in Brayden's back to take a kidney sample. It seemed extreme, and I wanted to avoid it at all costs. The doctor prescribed a round of antibiotics for Brayden and told us to call him if there was a third occurrence of blood in the urine.

As soon as he finished the two-week course of antibiotics, he went to school for three or four days and then somehow became reinfected with the strep, and we found blood in his urine again. We took him back to CHOP a third time and decided we needed to schedule the biopsy so they could officially diagnose the illness. The doctor said that it was highly probable there was a child in Brayden's first-grade class that was a strep carrier and asymptomatic. Since Brayden had sensitivity to the bacteria, after the antibiotics were out of his system he would become reinfected in school again. Having him on antibiotics constantly was also a stress on the kidneys, but in order to treat the IgA nephropathy we had to have the diagnosis. The whole situation was overwhelming, and I felt like a bundle of nerves because I couldn't control what was happening. As a mother, I just wanted to fix it and make it go away, but I couldn't and I felt helpless. We scheduled the biopsy for one week out; Brayden would miss two days of school for it.

When we got home I went for a five-mile run to clear my head. I began running at age eleven in middle school and never stopped. It became a way for me to settle my mind and relax. If something overwhelmed me, I could run a few miles and work it out in my head; it grounded me, and on this day I needed it desperately. It was my first time running since Briella's birth seven weeks earlier, so I ran at an easy, gentle pace. As I jogged through the developments under the streetlights, I organized the process of Brayden's illness. Tears ran down my cheeks in line with my stride, but the night's darkness kept me hidden. It felt good to let it go and run it out. By the time I got home, I could barely catch my breath, both from my pace and the emotions that pounded my chest. I walked around the block a few times to breathe deeply and settle myself. I felt ready to handle the biopsy and whatever results it yielded.

Only one person was allowed in the room during the biopsy. I decided it would be better for Brayden's father to stay, since I couldn't be in the room without crying and possibly scaring my son. They sedated him, and I kissed and hugged him. Then my dad gave him a hug and a kiss, too.

"See ya, Mommy," he said, giving me the thumbs-up. I winked and blew him a kiss as I headed for the waiting area. My dad went to the hospital chapel and said some prayers. About a half hour later, my dad came into the waiting area with some books under his arm. He had stopped at the hospital bookstore and picked up some gifts for Brayden.

"Your eyes are all red. Are you getting sick?" he asked.

"Umm...I've been crying," I replied, but I wanted to say, "Way to be a caveman!"

"Let's go for a walk to the cafeteria," he said. My father was a cafeteria connoisseur. He loved the limitless food options and the ability to eat anything at any time; it was the same reason why he loved diners. Although I wasn't the least bit hungry, I decided to take the walk with him to break up the waiting room monotony. My father, clearly unaffected by the stress of the situation, was amazed at the variety of delicacies. He got a tray of food while I sat at a table in the corner and cried. He urged me to eat but I couldn't; my stomach felt sick, and I wouldn't feel good again until I could see my little boy smile and hear his happy voice. My dad tried to make small talk and cheer me up, but I preferred silence while waiting for the call to tell me everything was okay. A short while later, I got the call on my cell phone. He was in recovery and I could go up and see my boy.

Brayden was sitting up, laughing, when I walked in the room. I hugged him tightly in my arms and kissed both sides of his cheeks.

"How are you, my love bug?" I asked.

"Good," he replied with a big smile. My dad walked over to him and hugged and kissed him and handed him the art activity books he had bought in the bookstore. Brayden's eyes lit up as he touched the colorful slabs of clay in an art book.

"Thanks, Papa," he said. My father smiled and hugged him again. They moved Brayden to a room where he would stay overnight, complete with video-gaming stations and a slushy machine at the end of the hall. Brayden thought he was in heaven. The hospital really did a great job of catering to the comfort of the children and their families. Once he was settled, I kissed him, gave him lots of hugs, and told him that I would call before bed. I said that I would see him the next morning. Only one person could spend the night with him. We decided his dad would spend the night with Brayden at the hospital, and I drove home with my father to nurse and take care of Briella. We promised to leave the house bright and early the next morning to pick them up at the hospital by 9:00 a.m. As we walked toward the elevators, I felt torn leaving the hospital without my boy. Part of me was staying there with him and part of me had to go home and take care of my other baby.

I didn't say much on the ride home. I looked out the window and cried a lot.

"Why are you crying? He's fine," my dad said.

"I feel like he's slipping through my fingers like grains of sand and I can't catch him and hold him there," I said tearfully, looking down at my open palm.

"Don't think the worst; just take it as it comes! You need to have faith!" my dad said. I wiped my tears away and nodded my head. He was right. I had placed myself in a negative Debbie Downer place and needed to climb back up into a positive space. I focused on letting go and sending positive energy to Brayden.

For the rest of the car ride home, I beamed energy from my third eye and right hand to his aura. I saw it enveloping him safely in a soft white blanket of light.

I was happy to see Briella when I got home. My mother said she had been a peaceful angel the whole time. I nursed and snuggled her a bit, then I put her in my bed with me. I couldn't sleep that night, so I sat up in bed and sent Brayden some more energy for his highest intentions. Between Briella's birth and Brayden's acute illness, I had forgotten that I could help him heal himself. I felt the warm energy soothing him, and I knew he was sleeping peacefully.

The next morning we went back to the hospital. I was so happy to see Brayden's bright eyes when I entered the room. Of course he was sad about leaving the hospital and the video games because he was beating his dad in a game of NHL. He had three slushies that night, so, to him, the hospital visit had been like an overnight party.

When Brayden came home I had a little celebration with the family. Everyone bought him small gifts. We were celebrating him being a big boy in the hospital. He loved it mostly because I went to Dairy Queen and got him a big mint chocolate chip ice cream cake. But I also think he liked that everyone made a big deal of him because Briella had been the focus for the last couple of months. It was a good way to end the hospital visit and divert our attention from the impending biopsy results.

The biopsy confirmed the IgA antibodies in Brayden's kidneys. Now the doctors could officially diagnose and treat the illness. Brayden returned to school, and within a few days he had blood in his urine again. We took him to CHOP and they suggested removing the tonsils, since he had had seven strep infections in five months. They hoped that removing the tonsils would prevent further strep infections and hence remove the trigger for the IgA nephropathy. I was nervous about the surgery because it involved anesthesia. Brayden had never had it, and I didn't know how his body would react, but given the circumstances and the acute nature of the strep and IgA nephropathy, we really didn't have an alternative. We scheduled the surgery with CHOP.

When we got home I set my healing table up in the living room and had Brayden recline on it. I placed my hand on the top of his head and just let the energy flow. He said he could feel heat coming into his head and his face felt hot.

"I like when you give me energy, Mommy." As I worked on his head I could hear his thought patterns. I heard, "If they don't want me anymore, maybe I can go live with Papa and Nana." I tried to just listen without being attached, but it was impossible; tears slipped out from my eyes. I quickly wiped them away because I didn't want Brayden to see. I also heard, "What if they don't love me anymore and what if they like her better?" I had to address these fearful thoughts.

"Brayden, are you thinking about living with Papa and Nana?" I asked.

"Well, I thought you don't need me anymore since you have the new baby, so maybe they'll let me live with them," he said matter-of-factly. At that point I realized that I hadn't covered all the bases with easing his transition to being a big brother. I had to deal with my failure and personal pity party at a later time.

I recentered my thoughts on the task at hand: helping Brayden heal his illness.

"Sweetie, we always want you here; you're a big part of this family."

He smiled at me and nodded his head. I needed to help him understand how he was making himself sick. His throat infection was ultimately all those things that he wasn't saying to us staying in there in anger. Energetically, the kidneys can store fears, and needless to say, based on his thoughts, he was feeling a tremendous amount of fear. I had to take these concepts and really break them down so he could understand how they were manifesting.

"Brayden, I want you to tell me whenever you're upset because if you keep it in there, then that angry energy stays in your throat and makes you sick."

"Is that why I keep getting sore throats?" he asked.

"Kind of," I said. I explained that he needed to tell me things and also let go of those fears. Our family had changed with Briella; it had grown and he needed to be part of it. I stood next to him and caressed his cheek gently with my fingertips.

"You're making yourself sick with this anger and these fears. All these negative thoughts are creating your illness. Do you understand what I mean?" I asked. He looked at me with his big bright eyes and nodded his head. I did feel that on a soul level he could comprehend it because he was born with his psychic and mediumship abilities activated and was clearly an old soul.

"I love you and want you here with us, but you have to want to be part of this family. You have to want to stay here and let go of all of this," I said. It pained my heart to say those words because I was admitting a complete lack of control in Brayden's healing. As a mother, I wanted to wave a magic wand and whisk his illness away, but it wasn't mine to heal. The only thing I could do was inform him of the root cause, help him release it, and give him unconditional love.

"Okay, Mommy. I'm stayin' here," he said with a big smile. I leaned down and hugged and kissed him. He gave me a frog kiss, which involved a big lick on my cheek; he had a few different kisses he would give me depending upon his mood. I told him that I would attune him to Reiki 1 so he could give himself energy whenever he wanted. After I attuned him, I explained about the chakras and hand positions. I didn't go into too much detail with him, but I taught him to work through all the chakras aligned with his spine so that he could balance himself. I let him know that he could tune in to the energy whenever he felt the need.

The day of the tonsil surgery Brayden was in good spirits, but nerves buzzed and stung inside me like bees inside a hive. When we walked into the hospital I clutched his hand tightly, as though it were the last time I would ever hold it. In the hall there was a teen boy in a wheelchair—his leg in a cast and his head hairless from his treatment. Our eyes met, and in his I saw the wisdom of a very old soul. A smile grew out of the corner of his lips, though I could feel the pain he carried. I think he sensed my apprehension, which was most likely written across my face like a billboard. I smiled back and sent him a healing thought. As I looked into his eyes, I knew he accepted his fate with courage and had a deep understanding of his journey; a soul is a soul regardless of the body that houses it.

We rushed into the busy pre-op room and signed in while they got Brayden comfortable in a bed. I filled out some insurance forms while Brayden played on his handheld gaming device for a few minutes, and then they wheeled his bed to the surgical room. When he was gone, I prayed that he would be okay. We collected our belongings, took our seat in the waiting room, and anticipated the receptionist's call to tell us he was out of surgery. Anxiety hovered over the room like a dark storm cloud waiting to pour down rain. Most of the parents were going through the same thing, and collectively the energy was intense and overwhelming. I placed myself in a big pink bubble and settled into writing. Having my laptop there so I could write gave me a way to disconnect and tunnel into my safety cocoon of what was familiar and secure. Within two hours the receptionist called us over and said she got the call that he was out of surgery and was fine. The surgeon would meet with us shortly in a meeting room. A few minutes later we were called into the meeting room, and the surgeon told us Brayden did fine. He was in recovery and we should be getting a call in about half an hour to be reunited with him.

We went back to the waiting room and awaited the call. A half hour came and went. I went over to the receptionist and asked her to check on him, and she said we would be getting called soon. An hour went by and still nothing. I went up to the receptionist and demanded to see my son. I told her I was not leaving the desk until someone came to escort me back to see Brayden. I had a terrible feeling in my sacral chakra, and I knew something was wrong.

Within a few minutes a nurse came back and led us to the recovery area. She said Brayden had woken up from the anesthesia; he was upset and calling for me. I quickened my pace and the nurse followed suit. She led me to a room with a glass sliding door, and when I slid it open Brayden reached out for me and called my name in a voice I could barely recognize. I sat on a chair next to his bed and the nurse placed him on my lap. I ran my fingers gently through his hair and talked in a calming tone. I told him that everything was fine; we were there with him and he wouldn't be left alone again. I assured him that it was all over. He had his arms around my neck in a vice grip and was gasping for air. I told him that he should stop trying to speak and should just relax. His erratic breathing concerned me.

Brayden was frightened out of his mind, so I knew something had happened. I asked the nurse why he was so scared. She said that after the surgery Brayden woke up as they were taking the breathing tube out of his throat and became scared. I tried to remain calm because I didn't want to upset Brayden further, but I felt a raging volcano in my chest ready to erupt in angry words. I took a deep breath and pushed the rage down to my feet.

I asked why they had waited an hour to bring me back there to him when he was asking for me. He was clearly anxious, so why would they delay reuniting him with me? She said that they were trying to relax him. A short man entered the room wearing green scrubs, a white jacket, and a shiny stethoscope around his neck. He introduced himself as the anesthesiologist. I immediately asked him why my son couldn't talk right, as his voice was barely discernable. The doctor looked at me and very calmly said there had been a slight complication with the surgery. So they had pulled the breathing tube out when Brayden was awake and they had a "slight complication"? I was thinking that the surgery sounded more like a train wreck rather than a routine procedure. The anesthesiologist said that they had initially put a breathing tube down his throat that was too large and they had replaced it with a smaller one, but they might have damaged Brayden's larynx in the process. They wouldn't be able to tell until a while after recovery. I couldn't contain the erupting volcano in me as the man stood in front of me talking about damaging my son's larynx like it was a scrape on his knee.

"I need to speak to you outside," I said to him in a very kind tone.

I handed Brayden to his father. I assured my son that I would be right back and that I was just going to talk to the doctor right outside the glass door so he could tell me what a brave boy Brayden had been in the surgery. I followed the doctor outside the glass slider door and closed it behind me, but I made sure Brayden could see me the whole time.

Suffice it to say that I didn't see eye-to-eye literally or figuratively with the anesthesiologist and his casual response to Brayden's post-operative condition. I inquired about the hospital's protocol for an issue between a doctor and parent that couldn't be resolved. He said his manger was unavailable, so I demanded to speak with a hospital department administrator immediately. Although he did not call an administrator, a nurse from the nearby nurses' station came over and said a director was on her way. I thanked her for her help.

Within five minutes a thin woman in white pants and a white lab coat with her dark hair styled neatly in a bob came over. She extended her hand and introduce herself as a department director and immediately asked, "How can I help?" I explained what had happened in Brayden's surgery and my concerns that he couldn't breathe and was having tremendous anxiety. I was also concerned about how all of this would affect his body, including his heart. The anesthesiologist remained silent. She instructed the anesthesiologist to give Brayden something to settle him and said they were moving him to intensive care for constant monitoring. The anesthesiologist fidgeted nervously as the nurses prepared Brayden's bed to be moved to the top floor. In the meantime, Brayden rested peacefully.

As soon as we exited the elevator and they wheeled Brayden's bed down the hallway to the intensive care unit, I felt the sadness imprinted on the walls like tiny remnants of each patient and parent who had ever stayed there. We passed rooms with sick children of all ages, some of whom were fighting for their lives. In the room next to Brayden's was a mother with a small baby in a crib. The side rail was down and the mother rested her head on the mattress next to the sleeping angel. There was a sense of despair in her limp body resting against that of her little one. Although I know on a soul level that babies who incarnate with illness and leave the earth shortly after have soul lessons and sign on for that experience, as a mother it was heart wrenching to see another mother going through that trauma, her heart torn and tattered from the journey. As I continued walking down the hall I focused the energy from my third eye and heart chakras and sent a tornado of light to the mother and asked that the energy in it be filled with whatever she needed to support her highest intentions.

Brayden's bed was rolled into his bright room. The entire left side was made of glass from floor to ceiling. There was a sofa on one side of the room and they brought in a reclining chair so we could sleep in the room with him. I guess the rules were different in the intensive care unit because we were both allowed to stay the night with him. Honestly, I would have thrown a fit if they wanted one of us to leave; I wasn't leaving my son's side. We were up pretty much the whole night. The nursing staff came in and checked on him what seemed like every fifteen or twenty minutes. Brayden had pain and there was also new anxiety. Every time he opened his eyes he would panic and reach for me. It was clearly the worst night of his life. I told him he was fine and I wasn't leaving him. The surgical experience had created an emotional scar that would have to heal. We had just gone through one illness, and now we would have to heal this emotional one. Each time he woke up he was reliving the trauma of the surgery, as though it played over and over in his mind like a video clip.

Brayden made it through the night without any real complications, so the next day they moved him from intensive care down to a post-operative floor. As they wheeled his bed to the new floor, a woman's voice came over the loudspeaker, calling, "Any available cardiologist to the cardiac resuscitation unit, STAT." My heart skipped as I realized someone's child might leave the earth at that moment. I focused my intentions, sent light to the child's parents for their highest intentions, and tightly held onto the side of Brayden's bed.

He was a little better on the new floor and began to relax. I got books from the library at the end of the hall and read to him during the night. I told him a Monkey Brayden story in an attempt to lift his spirits. Monkey Brayden was a fictional little brown monkey we had created and told stories about each night. He was kind of like Curious George, but he was a little crazier—he would put our dogs in my car and drive them to Dairy Queen to get vanilla cones. Sometimes Brayden was in the stories and would try to talk Monkey Brayden out of his crazy schemes, but that silly monkey was headstrong, and once he decided on a scheme there was no stopping him. Sometimes I would tell the story and other nights Brayden would make it up. The narratives always had happy, funny endings and left an open end for Monkey Brayden to continue his adventures in another story. But this night even Monkey Brayden couldn't put a smile on my little boy's face.

The nephrologist came in and checked on him, and so did the surgeon who had performed the tonsillectomy. Brayden was happy to see these smiling faces. The doctors kept him overnight again, just to make sure that he was okay. Brayden woke up constantly, feeling scared and having panic attacks. I comforted him and put him back to sleep. I really felt anger toward the anesthesiologist. Clearly, waking up while they were pulling the breathing tube out of his throat had been a horrifying experience for Brayden. He was released the following day, and we went home. I hoped that he would sleep better in his own bed.

The first night home he woke up three times, crying my name and panicking. Although his voice was coming back, which meant they had not damaged his larynx, he was having a post-traumatic stress reaction to the surgery. I slept on his floor and told him I wouldn't leave him. That continued every night for the first week home. I knew I would have to energetically work with him and help him release that fear imprint and active memory that kept replaying in his mind like a broken record skipping on the same spot.

In the meantime, I also felt that the situation with Brayden needed to be addressed by the hospital. Procedures hadn't been followed properly, and as a result Brayden was having an emotional issue. I wanted the hospital to not only address it, but also to fix it, so that no other child had to experience what Brayden was going through. I had no intention of suing or doing anything else that was karmically inappropriate, but this was an opportunity to make a positive change that would help other people. If we witness the problem, we should be part of the solution.

One night I sat and wrote a chronological narrative of the events to the president of the hospital and also the hospital's director of quality. CHOP was run like a well-oiled machine, and most of their quality documentation was listed on their website. I suggested that they change the policy so if a child is under duress, they bring the parents back immediately to ensure that child's emotional security. I FedExed the information to the CHOP president, and within a week I received a letter from the hospital stating that they were reviewing and making changes to the post-operative procedures, and I would be getting a follow-up letter with the policy changes within thirty days.

In addition, the anesthesiologist called me and apologized. He offered to arrange counseling at the hospital for Brayden with one of their staff psychologists. Although the gesture was honorable, it was not feasible due to the driving distance. I reminded him that every time he went into surgery, parents trusted their child's life in his hands. I felt it was important for him to remember that what was ordinary and routine for him involved the safety and security of a child's life each time he went into that surgery room. He agreed and gave me his cell phone number and told me to call him if I needed anything else. I thanked him for the call and wished him well. I let go of any angry feelings I held in my energy for him and the situation. It was a learning and growing experience for us both.

A few weeks later I got a follow-up letter from the hospital's quality department. They had changed the post-operative procedure. If there was some type of complication, the protocol was changed so the parents would be brought back to the child immediately. I also received a flow chart for the written quality procedure. I felt that was a positive change so no one would go through what we experienced. I was also happy that the hospital listened and made the change. We had taken a bad situation and collaborated to turn it into a good one. Sometimes things happen with us present because we're supposed to be part of the change.

I energetically worked on Brayden every day after that point, and he also worked on himself as he healed. He was quite comfortable working with the energy. I had attuned him to the Reiki Master level and he emerged as a profound healer. He didn't have any further kidney issues after the tonsillectomy, and his IgA nephropathy was and still is considered in remission. At the young age of six, he had acknowledged and cleared the root of the illness, so he prevented any further manifestation. I encouraged him to work on himself daily for ten to fifteen minutes so he would balance his energy regularly.

In hindsight, I realize Brayden's illness was meant to happen at that time. Brayden needed to remember how to use his healing abilities and work with the divine energy early on in his life. He was on track with his healing. I knew it would serve him well in the future. I still sometimes ask him for energy when I feel tired or have him scan me. His energy is always warm and loving yet intense, and he can see inside the body and feel where the energy is going, just like me. To this day, he and his sister, Briella, are the only people on the earth plane that give me hands-on healing. He's an old soul in a young body and engages all his tools in this life.

EXERCISE
Balancing the Chakras

Energy is everything. It's in us and all around us. Sometimes we need to balance the energy in us as things change and shift in response to what's going on around us. The shifts can be subtle over a long period of time or dramatic based on our relationship to the experience. Either way, shifts need to be aligned and balanced.

Chakras are energy centers in our bodies. The primary seven chakras are in line with the center of the body, from the base of the spine to the top of the head. They govern the physical aspects of the body where they are located, and each chakra also has some metaphysical attributes as well. When a person's body is healthy, all chakras are aligned and spinning properly. In an unhealthy body, wherever there is a manifestation of illness, the coordinating chakra that governs the area of physical manifestation is also misaligned.

Everyone has hand chakras in the centers of their palms. We all have the ability to balance the energy in our bodies using our own hand chakras. This chakra-balancing exercise is a great way to align your energy in just five minutes. In an optimum situation it should be done daily, but at a minimum it should be done once a week. The exercise is a simple one that not only aligns and balances but also centers and relaxes your energy.

As you balance the energy centers using your hand chakras, you may feel physical sensations associated with your energy shifting. You may feel heat or cold, tingling sensations, or pulsating. All of these experiences are normal sensations associated with the energy moving in your body; you may feel one or all of them, depending on your level of clairsentience. This psychic ability enables us to perceive energy through feeling. We can feel the energy of other people or the energy in a place.

When we work from the top of the head down the body, we are bringing the energy down and settling ourselves. When we are working from the root chakra up to the head, we are increasing the energy flow upward. If you feel stressed or anxious, you will want to balance your energy from your head down to your feet. If you feel lethargic, you will want to bring the energy up from the root chakra to the crown.

Here is an overview of the seven chakras:

Seventh Chakra

NAME: crown chakra

LOCATION: top of head

COLOR: pearly white (sometimes violet)

GOVERNING AREA: pineal gland, brain

ATTRIBUTES: center for spirituality and our connection
to the divine source

Sixth Chakra

NAME: third eye or brow chakra

LOCATION: center of forehead

COLOR: indigo

GOVERNING AREA: pituitary gland, physical eyes, center for clairvoyance

ATTRIBUTES: our ability to see things clearly, both physically and psychically

Fifth Chakra

NAME: throat chakra

LOCATION: center of the throat

COLOR: crystal blue/silver

GOVERNING AREA: throat, nose, ears, sinuses, thyroid gland

ATTRIBUTES: center of physical communication; speaking up for ourselves, speaking our truth; houses three psychic senses: telepathic or clairaudient communication, clairgustance, and clairscent/clairalience

Fourth Chakra

NAME: heart chakra

LOCATION: center of the chest

COLOR: emerald green

GOVERNING AREA: heart, immune system, thymus gland, upper lobes of the lung

ATTRIBUTES: center of compassion and unconditional love for ourselves and others

THIRD CHAKRA

NAME: solar plexus

LOCATION: just below the sternum

COLOR: yellow

GOVERNING AREA: upper digestive tract: stomach, liver,
gallbladder, pancreas, and spleen; skin, nerves, lower
lobes of the lungs

ATTRIBUTES: sense of identity, personal power

SECOND CHAKRA

NAME: sacral chakra

LOCATION: two inches below the naval

COLOR: orange

GOVERNING AREA: sexual organs, bladder,
upper intestines

ATTRIBUTES: this is our center for creative energy as well as
our main area for sexual energy and our emotions; it is
also the center for our clairsentient abilities

FIRST CHAKRA

NAME: root or base chakra

LOCATION: at the base of the spine in the pelvic region

COLOR: red

GOVERNING AREA: lower intestines, skeletal system,
legs, feet

ATTRIBUTES: related to security, survival, and our
connection to the earth

What you will need for this exercise: the palms of your
hands, a bed or sofa to recline on

• • • •

Recline flat on your back. You may place a pillow
under your head for comfort.

Relax your breathing. Breathe in to the count
of three and out to the count of three. Do this five
times. Feel your body relax deeper with each breath.

Place one of your palms at the top of your
head. Feel the energy there as you connect your
hand chakra with your crown chakra. It might feel
warm or you may sense a spinning sensation in
your palm. What you feel depends on your level of
clairsentience. Allow the energy to balance there for
a minute, until you feel it fitting under your palm
and spinning in a clockwise direction. When the
energy is spinning clockwise, this means the chakra
is moving in the right direction. A chakra spinning
counterclockwise means the chakra is out of balance
and can also mean a person is giving out too much
energy from this area. A balanced, aligned chakra
should fit nicely under the palm of the hand, have
a vibrant color, and spin in a clockwise direction. If
any of these attributes are not present, the chakra
needs healing.

Keeping one hand on the top of your head, gently
place your other palm on the center of your forehead, over your third eye/brow chakra. Using your
intention, send the energy from your crown chakra
down to your brow chakra. Keep both hands in

place until you can feel the energy pulsating in the brow chakra.

Remove the hand from the top of your head and place it by your side. Keep the other hand over the brow chakra. Allow the energy to balance there for a minute, until you feel it fitting under your palm and spinning in a clockwise direction.

Once you sense that it is balanced, keep one hand over the brow chakra and gently place the other over the throat chakra, in the center of your throat. Using your intention, send the energy from the center of your forehead down to the throat. Keep both hands in place until you can feel the energy pulsating in your throat chakra.

Remove the hand from your brow chakra and place it by your side. Keep the other hand over the throat chakra. Allow the energy to balance there for a minute, until you feel it fitting under your palm and spinning in a clockwise direction.

Once you sense that it is balanced, keep one hand over the throat chakra and gently place the other over the heart chakra, in the center of your chest. Using your intention, send the energy from the center of your throat to your heart chakra. Keep both hands in place until you can feel the energy pulsating in your heart chakra.

Remove the hand from your throat chakra and place it by your side. Keep the other hand over the heart chakra. Allow the energy to balance there for a minute, until you feel it fitting under your palm and spinning in a clockwise direction.

Once you sense that it is balanced, keep one hand over the heart chakra and gently place the other one over the solar plexus, located where the rib cage splits. Using your intention, send the energy from the heart down to the solar plexus. Keep both hands in place until you can feel the energy pulsating in the solar plexus.

Remove the hand from your heart chakra and place it by your side. Keep the other hand over your solar plexus. Allow the energy to balance there for a minute, until you feel it fitting under your palm and spinning in a clockwise direction.

Once you sense that the energy is balanced, keep one hand over the solar plexus and gently place the other one over the sacral chakra, just below the navel. Using your intention, send the energy from the solar plexus down to the sacral chakra. Keep both hands in place until you can feel the energy pulsating in the sacral chakra.

Remove the hand from your solar plexus and place it by your side. Keep the other hand over the sacral chakra. Allow the energy to balance there for a minute, until you feel it fitting under your palm and spinning in a clockwise direction. Allow the energy to balance in this area under your palm.

Once you sense that the energy is balanced, keep one hand over the sacral chakra and gently place the other one over the root chakra, at the base of the spine. Using your intention, send the energy from the sacral chakra to the root chakra. Keep both hands in place until you can feel the energy pulsating in the root chakra.

Remove the hand from your sacral chakra and place it by your side. Keep the other hand over the root chakra. Allow the energy to balance there for a minute, until you feel it fitting under your palm and spinning in a clockwise direction.

Once you sense that the energy is balanced, place both hands on the top of your head, at your crown chakra. Feel the energy from the crown pulsating under both palms. Using your intention, send the energy from the crown down to the feet. When the energy reaches the feet, send it back up to the crown. Concentrate on sending the energy between the crown and feet four or five times. As you are doing this, you are completely balancing the energy in your entire body. When it feels that the energy is evenly distributed and flowing in a balanced rhythm, remove your hands from the top of your head and place them on top of your thighs.

Connect your palm chakras to the tops of your thighs and stand up, with both feet on the ground. Feel the pulsating energy between your hands and your thighs. Use your intention to send all the energy from your head down to your legs. When you feel it in your legs, send it down to your feet.

Next, feel the energy going from your feet into the ground. Sense the connection between your energy and the ground. Feel the solidity of the connection. When you feel this connection, you are deeply grounded and balanced.

• • • •

EXERCISE

Sending Energy Remotely

As you read in this chapter, I sent energy remotely to Brayden while he was in the hospital and I could not be present with him because I had to be home with Briella, who was a newborn at the time. We can send healing, light, love, positivity, energy, and thoughts to others remotely, even if we are not attuned to a modality of healing. When we are attuned to a modality of energy work, we are tapping in to the infinite universal life force energy that is all around us—basically, the divine Source. When we are attuned and send energy remotely, we are sending the energy that is around us and not using our own personal energetic resources. When we are not attuned to an energetic modality of healing and we send energy to others or to a place remotely, we are using the energy within us. It is fine to do this, but you can become drained energetically, especially if you are emotionally attached to the person you are sending to.

When we send energy to others or places remotely, we must always send it for whatever is in the highest intentions of the recipient. We do not want to ever send energy with our intentions because we do not want to ever impose our will on the free will of others; we are not privy to all the karma and soul agreements of others, and therefore we cannot say what is in their highest interests. For example, a person may be terminally ill and you may want to send energy to that person. If you say, "I send this energy so that she will heal her illness," then by sending energy with this intention, you are putting stipulations and limitations on that energy. Maybe that person will not heal her illness. Maybe she is healing spiritually through that illness. If the energy is sent for her highest intentions, then her guides will use that energy for whatever is in her soul's best interest.

The same holds true for sending energy to a place. We may want to send energy to a place where a natural disaster has occurred, for instance. You would send the energy for the collective highest intentions of everyone there or you could just send light and love for whatever is needed there.

What you will need for this exercise: a quiet space and
 your mind in a relaxed state

· · · ·

Sit comfortably and close your eyes. Shield your energy in a protective bubble of whatever color makes you feel safe. Set your intention for the energy you will send, including the recipient and what you are sending, such as love, light, healing, etc.

Envision the person you wish to send the energy to. Once you see them in your mind's eye, place your hands up, palms facing away from you, and feel the energy flowing from your heart chakra, in the center of your chest, and down your arms and out your hands. Allow the energy to flow until you feel that it is no longer being accepted. Once you are done sending the energy, place your hands on your thighs and send all the energy in your body from the top of your head and down to your feet. When you feel the energy pulsating in your feet, you are grounded. You can release the bubble that you used, as well.

• • • •

3

The Fight of His Life

My brother Kyle, a notorious wise-ass, was only twenty-six when he sat on my sofa one night and blurted out "I think I got ball cancer" in a jocular tone. As usual, I thought he was joking, so I laughed it off and continued folding laundry.

"Very funny, geek," I said. We always referred to each other as geek, nerd, etc. Teasing was a sign of affection between us.

"I'm serious," he replied as he shifted the baseball hat on his head. He described a constant dull ache in his left testicle while cupping his crotch area. I said that he had probably pulled his groin playing basketball and asked him to stop touching himself like a freak in my den. He laughed and then we switched topics.

Two weeks later Kyle visited his primary care physician to have it examined. The doctor said it might be an infection, prescribed Kyle a round of antibiotics, and as a precaution sent him later that day for an ultrasound. Kyle went for the ultrasound and was told that his doctor would call him with the results. The ringing phone woke Kyle at 8:00 a.m. the next morning. The primary care physician's voice uttered words that Kyle wasn't prepared to hear. He said that the ultrasound results showed a mass in the testicle but cautioned Kyle about overreacting, since they had yet to determine if it was benign or malignant. He referred Kyle to an oncologist and told him to contact that office right away because it might be a while to get an appointment. Kyle hung up the phone and immediately dialed the oncologist's office. He got an appointment for later that same day. The next five days would be a medical whirlwind for him.

The oncologist was close by in Monmouth County. A man with milky white skin that glowed against his contrasting black facial and head hair entered the room in a white lab coat and khaki pants. He introduced himself as the oncologist and extended his hand to Kyle, who towered over the man with his six foot two frame. Based on the scans, the doctor said that he was 99 percent sure the mass was cancerous and suggested removing the testicle completely rather than waiting for biopsy results. He referred Kyle to a urologist, who would perform the surgery. Kyle called the urologist and got an appointment two days later.

The urologist had kind eyes and a friendly smile that relayed his gentleness, and Kyle immediately liked his energy and felt comfortable with him. The urologist suggested that Kyle go to a sperm bank and freeze some sperm because the surgery could affect sperm production. At that point they thought the cancer was stage 1, so they scheduled the testicle removal surgery for two days out and a chest X-ray and PET scan the day before the surgery.

That night Kyle asked me to scan him. He was wearing a heavy sweatshirt and sweatpants and reclining on his former bed in our parents' house. The room was dimly lit by electric Christmas window candles that my mother left on the window-sill year-round because she said it gave the house a warm colo-nial look.

I raised my hands about six inches above him and moved them up and down the length of his body, silently scanning. I could see inside him like an X-ray; the muscles and organs were in black and white. Kyle's chest heaved as he breathed deeply, and I knew he had anxiety because I suddenly felt like I wanted to jump out of my skin. The testicle was totally black, and it looked like it had sharp, pointy spikes around it. When I moved my hand upward toward the lungs, I saw a couple of dark spots as well but not with the spikes, and I knew the cancer had spread to his lungs.

His breath shifted to short, quick inhales, and I wasn't sure if he was feeling the energy or if it was nervousness. I asked with my mind what level this cancer was at, and I heard "intermedi-ate." I also heard that he would face the fight of his life, and it would be very difficult for him.

Kyle, in his usual impatient character, kept asking me, "What are you finding? Why aren't you saying anything?" I really didn't want to tell him what I was sensing.

"Shut it! You're distracting me," I replied. He rolled his eyes and frowned at me. "It's just in the testicle," I said. I totally lied to him for two reasons: first, I didn't want to scare him, and sec-ond, I wasn't medically qualified to diagnose anyone. He settled his breath and I watched the muscles in his face relax. "You'll be fine, and besides—whatever comes your way, we'll get to the root of it and heal it; we're healers," I said. He nodded and said,

"Thanks, loser." I'd have to be on my deathbed for either of my brothers to say something affectionate and loving. Joking was our way of relating to each other.

I attuned him to Reiki 1 after I scanned him. I thought it would be a good tool for him to have, since Reiki 1 was about self-healing. I gave him an overview of the hand positions and a handout with all the Reiki 1 basics that he could read at the hospital.

The next day Kyle went to the hospital for the testicle removal surgery. It was a same-day surgery, which meant he would have the surgery in the morning and be released from the hospital later that same day. My other two siblings, parents, and Kyle's girlfriend hung out in the beige waiting room, sitting on stiff brown fabric-covered chairs, thumbing through magazines, and making small talk, trying to hide the collective nervousness. I sent Kyle energy a couple of times for whatever was in his highest intentions and visited the snack bar on the first floor with Brayden and Briella several times. Even though I had coloring, games, and books for them, they still needed to get up and move around to escape the boredom that invaded the waiting-room walls.

Kyle came out into the recovery room joking about still being able to make it with the ladies with one testicle. "This little guy's still gonna work, right, doc?" he asked, pointing to his crotch. "I gotta have my junk workin' for the ladies!" The doctor smiled and said that everything should be fine. Then he shook Kyle's hand, told him that he would see him in the morning, and swiftly exited the room. It was amazing that within five days Kyle had found out he had cancer, frozen his sperm, and had a testicle removed. His spirits were high and we all thought the worst was behind him.

The day after the surgery, Kyle returned to the urologist for the chest X-ray and PET scan results. The test results showed the cancer had spread to his lymph nodes and lungs. At that point it was considered stage 3A testicular cancer. The doctor said Kyle would need further treatment, which involved chemotherapy, and he would need to see the oncologist again to go over the specifics of the treatments and prognosis. Kyle wasn't prepared to hear that information. He was under the impression that after the surgery he would be fine.

Kyle called me on his way home from the urologist and shouted, "It's in my lungs. Is that why you spent so much time scanning my lungs? What else do you know? Why didn't you tell me the truth?" My heart dropped because I knew what I had seen when I scanned him, but hearing him on the phone made it all true. Even though I saw the cancer, it wasn't real until the doctors diagnosed it. Sadness mixed with nausea twisted in me and rose up my digestive tract like a gastric volcano. I sat down on a bench in my kitchen, cupped my forehead in my hand, and closed my eyes. I took a deep breath in and said, "I didn't tell you because I'm not a doctor and I'm not allowed to diagnose anyone. Plus I wasn't sure if it was accurate; I doubted myself with the information because I'm so emotionally attached to you."

"You're bullshit. You should've told me the truth. I'm not one of your clients; I'm your goddamn brother!" he said with anger. I bit down sharply on my lower lip until I tasted blood. I let him vent because I knew the sting of the diagnosis was painful, and his anger was less about my scan and more about the reality of facing advance-staged cancer.

After I hung up the phone, I got in my car and drove a couple of miles to the bay, to my favorite place. It's a little beach that I always rode my bike to when growing up—literally down the street from my parent's house. I pulled into the parking lot and sat for a moment, staring at the endless waves lapping upon the shore. I focused on the sun's luminous light reflected on the water. My mind was racing and spinning in all directions, like a top. For me, the beach had always been a grounding place. The second my feet touch the sand, I feel connected and centered. I needed that feeling after hearing that diagnosis.

I got out of the car and walked over to the shoreline. When I stepped on the sand I didn't feel very grounded, so I sat down. As soon as I felt the sand support my body, a single tear slipped out of my eye, and one by one they streamed down my face like a faucet. Then I just let them flow with short heaving breaths. I let the sadness and pressure escape, and as I watched the waves roll out to the bay, I sent my sadness and fears with them. Then I invited new energy to flow in from the waves and wash over me. I let the salt air balance and cleanse me, just as I always did in this special place.

I knew I needed to be strong for my little brother. I also recognized that he had to heal himself, but having a healing medium as a sister was certainly a valid weapon in his battle arsenal. As I sifted my fingers through the sand around me, my mind organized a process of how to help Kyle. I began writing words in the sand as they popped into my head one by one. I wrote the word *diet*. I knew he needed help with his diet, which consisted mostly of fast food with minimal nutritional content. Cancer thrived in an acidic body and would grow rapidly if fed by sugars. I could get him on a shot of organic green vegetable juice with kale, romaine, cilantro, garlic, cucumber, and lemon each morning on an empty stomach. It would probably provide more nutrients than his body had absorbed in a long time. I would get him to cut out all flour and sugar—bye-bye, processed foods. Next, I wrote the word *greens* in the sand.

I decided to work on his energy once a week and also ask my family members to send distance healing a few times over the course of his chemotherapy treatments. We had fifteen Reiki Masters in our family; it had to help. I wrote the words *weekly healing* and *distance healing* in the sand. I made a mental note of all the healing words I had written in the sand, and then I took a picture of them with the camera on my cell phone. I said a silent prayer asking to be guided to help my brother in the best way for his healing. Then I wiped the last of my tears, got in my car, and drove home.

Kyle wasn't comfortable with the local oncologist, so a family friend referred him to Memorial Sloan Kettering (MSK) in New York City. My mother called the hospital, and Kyle had an appointment for a consultation the following week.

At MSK a tall man with gray hair and thin-rimmed glasses entered the room and introduced himself as the oncologist. Both his inflection and the information he relayed conveyed his expertise in the field, and Kyle later told me that as soon as that doctor spoke, Kyle immediately felt like his life was in the right hands. The doctor reviewed the tests and said that Kyle would need intense chemotherapy, which involved four rounds. He would need five straight days of treatment for three hours each day and then be off for two weeks to recover. After the rounds of chemo, he would need surgery to remove all the lymph nodes from the testicle area up to the chest, in case there were dormant cancer cells hiding there. The doctor also said that Kyle might become infertile because chemotherapy could damage sperm, so he recommended that Kyle go to the sperm bank and make another deposit. Within four weeks he would begin his first round of chemotherapy. Kyle didn't know what to think. One minute he was a normal twenty-six-year-old man and within a couple of weeks he was diagnosed with an advanced form of testicular cancer and getting ready to begin chemotherapy.

The day before my brother was supposed to begin his chemotherapy we had a big dinner at my house. Kyle was a little down because he had worked his last night at the Bamboo Bar, where he bartended. I think he not only loved his job because he made friends with people from all walks of life but he also felt energized by the electric energy of the crowds. Not working for a while was going to be rough for him.

There were lots of laughs and teasing, as always, at my house that night. After dinner Kyle walked out the front door with my parents. I ran up and gave him a big hug.

"This is just a bump in the road. You got this!" I said.

"I know. I'm gonna kick cancer's ass," he said.

"Love you, buddy!" I said and kissed him on his cheek.

"Love you, too. See ya in a week, loser," he said as he turned and walked toward the car. I felt scared that he would have a struggle and I couldn't be there to help him. As soon as I got through the front door, my love bugs, Brayden and Briella, were waiting there to give me hugs; they always knew when I needed some love.

Midway through his first round of chemo, I was riding the stationary bike at the gym early in the morning when a tidal wave of nausea washed over me. It was morning sickness magnified a thousand times and carried a metallic taste in its wake. I seriously thought I would vomit on the gym floor. I didn't know what was going on, but I knew what I was feeling wasn't mine. I texted Kyle and asked how he was feeling.

"I was just about to text you. Please send me energy. I'm so nauseous and too sick to work on myself," he said. I explained to Kyle that I was feeling his nausea. He apologized for sending me the feeling; it wasn't intentional. I knew I had a strong energetic cord connection to Kyle, but this experience took it to a higher level and taught me a big lesson. If I was going to help him, I had to remember to cut the cord each day between us and shield my energy so I wouldn't feel his illness. I found a quiet corner of the gym by the stairs. I sat down, focused my mind, and sent my brother the energy he needed. When I was done, I made sure to ask Archangel Michael's help in cutting all cords between us so that I didn't feel the imprints of Kyle's energy. I'm glad I learned that lesson early on in his treatment so I didn't have to experience it the whole time.

The second round of chemo recovery was harder than the first one. Kyle remained in his room every day, lying in his bed, sipping Gatorade. His dark cave room had curtains drawn and felt cold, like a crypt. His yellow lab, Simon, rested at the foot of his bed religiously; he wouldn't leave Kyle. I remember walking into the room and looking at the dog and asking myself if

Simon was sick because he was acting like Kyle. He didn't even get off the bed to greet me. It was strange—like the dog could feel Kyle's cancer.

I would go over each day and sit by Kyle's bedside and give him energy. Most days I would hold his ankles, grounding him and pulling all the energy through his body. Some days he wouldn't say much and would just sleep, but I knew the energy was helping him. One of the days during that week, while working on him I silently asked what the illness was rooted in. I was told he had deep resentment of himself.

"Do you resent and hate yourself?" I asked.

"Kinda," he said. I really had never felt that way, so I didn't understand what he was talking about. "I mean, all you guys (the siblings) are successful, have money, good careers, and everyone graduated from college, and I'm just the loser in the family," he said. I was so surprised that he said that because I didn't view him that way. I saw him as just a kid that had to find his way in life—a goofy late bloomer.

"I'm twelve years older than you. Imagine what your life will be like in twelve years—completely different from where you are now! You can't compare yourself to me. It's like comparing an infant to a middle-schooler." He smirked. "It doesn't matter what your job is or how much money you have. It matters what kind of life you live and what you do for other people. You're awesome, and you need to see yourself that way!" I explained that he needed to work on self-acceptance and self-love to heal the cancer he created in his body. He said that he understood and agreed that he would work on it.

While Kyle had his third round of chemo, I was scheduled for an interview in New York City with a *New York Times* reporter. The interview was for a joint collaboration between Good Morning America and CafeMom. I had been selected to talk about being a mom entrepreneur.

Kyle was staying at the American Cancer Society's Hope Lodge in New York City on West 32nd Street. The Hope Lodge is an amazing facility that provides lodging at a minimal rate to cancer patients and their caregivers receiving outpatient care who have a one-hour or longer commute. Kyle's treatment was every day for five days, and the drive would have been too much for him each day. My mother stayed at a Marriott the first round with him and they gave her a discounted rate, but it was still $275 a night. The Hope Lodge was a beautiful, comfortable place for my brother and mother to stay, and honestly I don't know what they would have done if it wasn't for that special place.

I told Kyle that I would come uptown to visit him. After the interview I hailed a cab and headed uptown. The weather was sunny and warm, and the streets were lined with people. All the outdoor bars were packed because the World Cup was on. The US had beaten Algeria earlier that morning, so everyone was pumped. They were watching the Ghana vs. Germany game. As we stopped at red lights, we heard cheers from outside, and the energy was lively and happy.

The Hope Lodge was inconspicuously set in a busy part of the city. If I didn't know the building number, I would've walked right past it. Who would have thought that among the hustle and bustle of the city there was a building filled with people fighting for their lives?

The place felt peaceful with its neutral-colored walls and light furniture arranged in an open pattern. The receptionist called Kyle's room while I waited in the meditation room. When I entered the room I saw my paternal grandfather, Pops, in spirit standing over by the window. He said he was watching over Kyle. I knew that something was wrong because Pops seemed concerned. I walked around the room and paced a bit like a lion in a cage. The pacing kept my body moving at the same rate as my worried mind. The room captured a lot of natural light with two walls full of windows, despite the fact that we were in a high-rise building in NYC. Kyle opened the partial glass door and asked my mother to please wait outside. She looked bewildered but said okay and then took a seat in the lobby.

Kyle walked through the door and into the room. He had on gray sweatpants and a gray sweatshirt, both of which matched his pale ashen skin. He looked like a six foot two shadow. Kyle reclined on a plush chaise and rested his elbows on the chair's arms.

He looked up at me and said, "I don't want Mommy to hear this. I'm not gonna make it; I can't fight it anymore. I'm not coming home." He leaned his head back on the chair and pulled his sweatshirt hood over his head. I sat down beside him and held his hand.

"You have to do this. You haven't even lived yet; you've got this!" I said with determination.

Tears slipped down his cheeks and he hid his face in his hand. "Pops is here watching over you," I said.

"He's been here all day. I saw him when I was getting my treatment and then he followed me back here. He's watching over me," Kyle said. I was a little surprised that he knew why my grandfather had been there all day. I knew Kyle could see and sense spirits, but I was unaware that he could communicate with them as well. I didn't call attention to it, but I made a mental note of it to discuss at a later date. Honestly, I was glad that he could communicate with our loved ones. It was just another tie that bound us together; his abilities were like mine.

"The treatment's killin' me. I feel myself dying more each day," he said.

"Yeah, the cancer part is dying. But your soul is strong, and you can fight more. Either you work stuff out here or you take it with you on the other side and do the work there," I said, wiping his tears with my hand.

"I can't do it—I got nothin' left. I'm not gonna drink the fluids after the treatment, and I'm gonna go into cardiac arrest," he insisted. With intense chemotherapy treatment, patients are required to drink fluids to hydrate the body and also push the medicine through the body. If they don't, they can go into cardiac arrest. I heard hopelessness in his voice and felt his despair. He was choosing death. I felt like someone had stabbed me in the heart.

I hugged him close to me and pleaded, "Please stay with me; I need you. You're the only one in this family who really gets me. You promised you'd always be here for me. Our souls agreed to help each other in this life. You can't check out now!" Our family is ultra Catholic and super conservative. Kyle and I were the renegades that beat to our own drums. We couldn't be broken as long as we had each other. We were determined to be ourselves despite the stringent family structure. For a moment, we both hugged and cried and released the sadness within us.

"I love you, buddy," I said, handing him a tissue.

"Love you too, dork," he said, blowing his nose. Then I stood up and started balancing his energy. I sent energy from the crown chakra in his head down to his feet. He could feel the warmth and said that it made him feel relaxed. As I moved down his chakras, I showed him some techniques I use in the Soul-Centered Healing Method. Kyle was the only person that I showed this to; ironically, he had already been using the hand techniques with his own healing. I asked how he knew the hand techniques and he said he wasn't sure but he was doing it after all his chemotherapy treatments. He would pull out what wasn't needed and fill the space with light. When he shared this with me, it confirmed that we were kindred spirits. I believe we have the same abilities and that Kyle could be a healing medium if he chose to focus his energy there. As I made my way down to his feet, I pulled all the energy down and grounded him so that he would get out of his head and into his body. I also added some energy to the aura, as he needed all the help he could get. I reminded him that our family members would be sending him distance healing that night, so he needed to be resting.

"Dude, I got cancer and need two more days of treatment. Where ya think I'm goin'?" he said, smirking. I knew he was feeling better.

"So we're clear: you're staying, right?" I asked, looking into his glassed eyes.

"I'm staying," he said.

"You don't have to fight it alone. I'm with you every step of the way, and on the days you can't do it, I'll carry you to the finish line," I said, hugging him. Then we rose and exited the room. I waved to Pops as I closed the door, and he nodded and smiled at me. I knew I'd done my job. I was supposed to be in the city on that day to help my brother when he was at his weakest. Sometimes when we're weak, God sends us someone who reminds us of our strength. As I drove home from the city that night, I kept sending Kyle mental messages to keep fighting and keep going. I felt him growing stronger.

Later that same night, all my cousins and my son were sending energy to Kyle at the same time. We had emailed each other the week before, setting a date and time that worked for all of us since we were located in various time zones in the US. I sat on the leather sofa in the den and closed my eyes. When I felt the connection to my brother, I raised my hands slightly and began sending him energy for his highest intentions. About fifteen minutes into sending the energy, I was told that we needed to stop because that was all his energy field could handle at that time.

I texted Kyle and told him we had sent the energy and ended the session. He said he saw white light in his room hovering over him and he felt warm and then his body got very hot. He said it was a little overwhelming, and he thought he needed some rest to process it. I asked if we could send another session during his last round of chemo, and he gave us permission to do it in the future.

He pulled through his last round of chemo like a champ because it was the end. Once again, our family members sent him more distance healing, and I believe it helped him recover quickly. After his recovery he had one final step in his treatment. He needed all the lymph nodes in his chest removed. The doctor said that it was necessary because sometimes the cancer would lie dormant in the lymph nodes after chemo and then would resurface.

Kyle had the surgery and the scar to prove it, from the pelvic area up to the middle of his chest, like a gutted trout. It was a good move because he had eighty-two lymph nodes removed, and they found active cancer cells in three of them.

After Kyle's treatment, the Bamboo Bar held a giant fundraiser for him with lots of food, entertainment, and a huge auction. The Sean Kimerling Testicular Cancer Foundation (www. seankimerling.org) donated cancer shower cards to put in all the auction gift baskets and hang around the bar. The shower cards could be hung on a shower head and demonstrated self-exams for testicular cancer. The Bamboo Bar had sold over one thousand tickets to the event, so I thought it was a great time to make the captive audience aware of testicular cancer signs and symptoms. I not only added them to the wrapped gift baskets, but I taped them all around the bar, especially in the bathrooms and stalls.

That was the best day during Kyle's cancer experience. So many people came—from grammar school, from his college, and family members from other parts of the country flew in. There was so much love and happiness in the air. I remember that my brother had me count all the money from the night, and I just cried because I was overwhelmed by the generosity of people. I was so glad to be able to witness such a beautiful life-changing event where people come together and help each other. We need more of that kind of good karma stuff in the news! It's what life is really about—connecting with others and helping. When we do that, we all grow together and evolve.

As I was writing this chapter, we were planning a huge party for Kyle to celebrate his five years of being cancer-free. He's now considered in remission. So, yeah, I guess you can say Kyle *did* kick cancer's ass. He found out what he was made of and won the fight of his life.

Kyle's cancer taught me that even as healing facilitators, though we want to help those closest to us, it's always up to the individual whether or not they heal. We're not in control. We're there to assist and help when they need it, but we can't do it for them. All we really can do is love them.

EXERCISE

Clearing Your Energy at the Beach

Many of us enjoy visiting the beach for a vacation, and some of us are even lucky enough to live close to it. Although the beach is great in the summer, it also has some profound healing properties that we don't always acknowledge. Sometimes we feel drawn to it and we don't know why. But when we get there, our souls recharge and we find grounding and balance. The beach is a great place to heal yourself at any time of year.

If you live close to a saltwater beach, your nose is filled with the salty scent carried in the air the second you step on sand. You breathe it in as the salt element cleanses your sinuses and lungs, expelling any toxins in your respiratory system. When you swim in the water, the salt cleanses your body. If you have any cuts on your skin, it helps them heal. Salt has both cleansing and healing properties, and by spending time at the beach, you are offering your physical body opportunities to heal and cleanse deeply.

The sand texture feels soft and supportive under your feet as it grounds your energy. When you walk on the beach, you connect yourself deeply to the earth; you are fully present. All the cares that circle your mind dissipate, and you take in all the sights and sounds around you. Some beach sand contains grains of quartz, which is high vibration and enhances your energetic vibration. Walking on the beach and connecting with this energy can cleanse your aura and ground you.

The rhythmic wave patterns visually, mentally, and audibly relax us. Have you ever sat on the beach when you were upset about something and watched the waves? As you see the waves, your mind seems to unfold and you feel more calm. Hearing the waves lap onto the shore and softly wisp back to sea gently soothes the ears.

The overall high-vibrational beach energy draws us in. When we feel compelled to visit it, we must understand that it is a soul's call for healing. The surfers of the 1960s knew this well. Those soul surfers heard and understood the call of the ocean and recognized it was not just a place to visit but rather a place to connect on a soul level—a place of peace and balance. When you feel drawn to the beach, know that it is a call to your soul. Go there! Leave all earthbound thoughts behind you and support your soul!

What you will need for this exercise: Access to a beach that has waves, although the waves don't need to be big. The beach can be an ocean, bay, river, or lake. As long as it has some small waves, you can use it for this exercise.

· · · ·

Sit down on the beach facing the water, settle yourself comfortably in the sand, and close your eyes.

Breathe in the salt air. Let it fill your lungs deeply. As you inhale, feel the air cleansing your entire respiratory system of any impurities. Exhale slowly, releasing any old energy trapped inside you.

Repeat the inhale/exhale process five or six times slowly and consciously.

As you sit on this beach and watch the ebb and flow of the tide, raise your hands and place them over your heart chakra, in the center of your chest. Feel the life force energy pumping out of the heart to the rest of the body. Notice whether your heart rhythm is in sync with the waves of the water.

Observe the rhythm of the waves as they wash upon the shore. Stand and walk toward the shoreline. Gently place your hands in the water. Feel the cool liquid between your fingers. Allow each new wave to unlock a little piece of your energy that's been stuck. Maybe you have been trapped in emotional patterns. Perhaps you have been caught in repetitive thoughts. Maybe you have been in stagnant situations and relationships with other people.

As the waves flow away from the shore, send away any of these pieces that are no longer a fit for you; envision each fragment floating away from you as a puzzle piece flowing out to sea. Do this one piece at a time and use as many waves as you need to until all the pieces are sent out to the sea. See them wash away back to the water and be cleansed, healed, transformed. Watch as the water draws out everything that has been draining you.

When you feel you have removed all the broken pieces, focus once again on the waves rolling in toward you. Allow the water to bring clean, clear energy into your vibration. Feel the energy carried in the water's current. See the waves flow in and allow this energy to wash over you. Let it recharge and energize you.

At the water's edge place both feet in the shallow waves. Deeply connect to the endless flowing energy. Allow your energy to flow down from your head to your feet and connect to the sandy shoreline. Enjoy the sense of peace you have created for yourself.

• • • •

4

Healing and Sacred Agreements

We never know when we'll be called to help someone else, but we always need to be ready. My cousin Mary was diagnosed with early stage breast cancer at age fifty-four. She called right after she received the diagnosis and asked me to help her heal the disease.

"I'm gonna beat this," she said with determination and sincere strength in her tone. I felt the strong commitment she was putting out in her energy.

"I'm sorry to hear this news, but I'll help you in any way I can on this journey," I said. Mary would also be working with her sister and one of my cousins, both of whom were certified Reiki Masters, as well as trained in other alternative healing modalities. I set a time for Mary to come to my house during the day because she worked evenings as a bartender.

A week after her initial diagnosis, Mary arrived early one morning and I had the massage table set up in my living room. She greeted me with her usual warm smile and a gentle hug.

"Let's do this!" she said, high-fiving me.

"I'm in," I said and guided her toward the table. She reclined comfortably on her back and I put a pillow under her knees. As soon as I said the opening prayer, tears painted wet lines down her cheeks. She said that she could sense the energy and felt as though she was wrapped in a loving blanket. She may have been feeling the healing energy, but her older sister, Gail, was also present in spirit at the end of the table. Gail had died from breast cancer and was there to help out with the session. I relayed the visit information to Mary and she began sobbing with short heaving breaths.

Historically, Mary was known as the "family crier" because she could cry at the drop of a hat—weddings, births, and funerals. Actually, she was very sensitive and as I worked on her, I also learned that she was highly clairsentient and could feel energy very intensely. Sometimes when people feel their loved ones in a session, they cry for two reasons. First, they're overwhelmed by the energy of the loved one, which comes in a totally loving vibration, and second, feeling that soul's energy makes them realize how much they miss the connection. When our loved ones go to the other side, we kind of block out the feelings associated with missing them, otherwise we recapitulate those feelings every time we think of them. But when we connect to their energy it can be a bittersweet experience.

Mary said that she felt Gail there and was so happy to know that she was helping. I didn't know the specifics of Mary's cancer manifestation other than it was in the breast. But when I got to her chest, I could see it as a black ball with spikes around it. I could feel the heaviness of it, and it was drawing energy from my hand as well as a lot of Mary's own energy like a giant magnet pulling in a metal weight. I placed my hand about six inches above her chest and held the energy there. Mary said she could feel heat pulsing in her.

I tried to hold the energy there while scanning with my third eye. Using my mind, I asked what the illness was about; I was told that in her marriage she was giving so much love out and not getting much in return. This revelation struck me because I didn't know how to address it. I wasn't close enough with her to know the intricacies of her marriage. I asked the angels to guide me with loving words in relaying the session's information.

Toward the end of the session, I asked Mary about her husband, Shamus. She said he was fine, but as I looked into her green eyes, shadows of sadness peered through the tears that glassed them.

"If you're going to heal yourself, you have to be honest and face whatever patterns and experiences are rooted in the cancer," I said gingerly.

"I love him and I know he loves me, but it's hard," she said, shedding more tears. I rubbed her shoulder and told her that it would be okay. I moved my hands over the heart chakra, in the center of her chest. I noticed the energy in the heart center was moving in a counterclockwise direction, which energetically validated that she was giving out more love than she was getting back in her relationship; it was causing deep resentment. She was good at communicating and showing her love, but her spouse wasn't and she often felt unloved. I had to relay this information to her because she wanted to know why she had manifested the cancer. I gently shared the information in the most loving possible way. I told her what I heard and asked if she felt it was true. She sobbed heavily, only nodding her head to confirm. I handed her a few tissues and she wiped her tears. In this case, the crying was cathartic and allowed her to heal by releasing some of the emotions and energy she stored internally.

I silently asked what she needed to do to heal herself. I was given two options to relay to Mary. The first option was that she could leave the relationship, and the second was to stop giving so much of herself and to change her expectations for her marriage. When I relayed this information to her, Mary said that she couldn't stop giving love because that was who she is and it was her job to give Shamus love. She also said that she could never leave him because he would be on the streets. He had a serious alcohol issue and she felt that without her in his life, he would immerse himself in his drinking. I explained that I was being told that she needed to do one of the two to heal her illness. She said she'd think about it and decide what to do.

Before she got off the table, I attuned her to Reiki 1 so she could work on herself during her treatments. I thought it would empower her in her healing journey. I gave her a Reiki 1 manual and told her to read it when she had time. I offered to give her healing sessions each week and said I would always make myself available whenever she needed a session. She wanted to pay me and pulled her wallet out of her purse. I told her that I had a rule of never charging family members for any healing work. She said it made her feel uncomfortable to not pay. I told her to let go of what the ego was telling her and to just accept the healing energy.

Many other family members were helping Mary as well. Some of her nieces bought her a juicer so she could drink raw green juice each day. They also helped her customize a diet with healthy food options to eliminate sugar and processed food. My cousins in South Carolina and Georgia were regularly sending her healing energy. She had a lot of help; she just needed to decide to live differently, and that was a big task.

A few weeks later Mary came for another session. I had the table set up in the backyard under the flowering plum tree, since it was early spring. She loved the outdoors and her plants, so I thought being outside in the warm sun surrounded by nature could raise her vibration and help her heal. When we walked into the yard and she saw the table set up under the white flowering tree, her eyes lit up and she giggled like a little girl.

"This is amazing. I feel so relaxed here, and the smell of the blossoms is calming," she said. It was a beautiful, warm day and birds sang and chirped. Life's vibrancy was everywhere. I was happy to see that cheerful Mary smile I had recognized my whole life. Mary said she had been giving herself energy every couple of days. She said she fell asleep that way many nights because it relaxed her. I was thrilled to know she was tuning in to the Reiki energy. I asked how things were in her relationship, and she said they were getting better. Her energy definitely looked less gray and felt less heavy. I truly believed she was trying to heal herself.

After our healing session, she got off the table and I led her to the center of the yard. I asked her to take her shoes off so we could ground ourselves.

"Walking barefoot on grass is a great way to ground your energy," I said to Mary. I explained that grounding was a way to pull our energy down so it was distributed evenly in our bodies.

I told her that when we were ungrounded our energy was mostly in our heads, so we felt dizzy or flighty and scattered.

"Maybe that is why I love working in my gardens. I enjoy touching the dirt with my hands, and it just feels good to me," she said. I smiled at her, and we walked in a circle as the green blades tickled the soles of our feet. I could feel all my energy being pulled down to my feet.

"Do you feel grounded?" I asked Mary.

"I'm not sure what grounding feels like, but I feel good. My head is clear and I'm happy," she said, smiling.

"Good. That's great! Anytime your head feels like it's busy with too many things, just go outside and walk around barefoot in the grass. It will pull all your energy down so you don't have too much in your head."

Before she left, I gave her a Larimar pendant and earrings that I had bought on eBay for her. Larimar is a beautiful soft blue/green stone from the Dominican Republic. In addition to its aesthetically pleasing appearance, metaphysically it is said to help heal the heart and throat chakras as well as heal loving relationships between soulmates. I thought it would be helpful for her to have it since she was working on healing issues in her relationship with Shamus. When I gave it to her, she offered to pay; once again, I declined. I told her that she could never give me money for any healing sessions or items related to her healing. I felt it was my duty to help since she was in my family, and I was happy she allowed me to be part of her healing process. She put the necklace on right away. It hung right over her heart chakra in the perfect spot.

A few weeks later Mary returned, and although I had planned on the session being under the flowering plum tree, it started drizzling, so I moved the table to the covered cabana next to my pool. It still afforded us the opportunity to enjoy the fresh air without getting wet. Halfway through the session, the rain pelted against the cabana roof in a rhythmical pattern, playing a gentle melody. It soothed Mary like a lullaby, and she fell asleep while I continued pulling all her energy down. I saw that she was still struggling with her relationship. It looked like she was trying to make changes, but Shamus wasn't flowing with them. The disease was progressing; this was a big difference since her last session with me.

I continued giving her energy and then I grounded her. As I pulled all the energy down through her feet, she woke up—perfect timing. She said she felt totally relaxed and peaceful and couldn't believe she had slept through the whole session. The rain had stopped, though a cloud-covered canopy hovered over our heads. I didn't tell her that I knew she was still struggling with her relationship. I figured that if she shared it, I would comment on it, but I wouldn't initiate it. Plus, since the information had come up as she slept in the session, I felt she was just supposed to receive the energy and I wasn't intended to communicate anything to her. She knew from the first session that the illness was rooted in her relationship, and she knew what she had to do to release it. She did say that she was still balancing her own energy, especially after her cancer treatments. I gave her a hug and told her to call me anytime she wanted energy or even if she just wanted to talk. I handed her a 5x4-inch piece of rose quartz and explained that the stone had a loving vibration and could be used to elevate the vibration of love in a space. I told her to put the stone in a room where she and Shamus spent the most time. She said she would leave it on the table in the den, right next to the television.

About four months after the initial diagnosis, we attended a benefit for Mary at the River Rock Café in Point Pleasant, NJ, where she had been a bartender for most of her adult life. The owners generously provided the venue and all the food and beverages. Many of Mary's friends and coworkers worked the event, from selling raffle tickets and T-shirts to serving. There was a lot of love and joy in the air. I donated a couple of baskets from my organic personal care company that I had at the time, and several family members donated items for the auction as well.

It was great to see Mary happy and smiling that day—so much positivity. I wished every day could be like that for her. I hadn't seen Mary's husband, Shamus, in some time, and I didn't recognize him at first. He had aged dramatically through the deep creases on his face and his completely graying hair. I didn't know if it was from alcohol or the stress of dealing with Mary's illness. Either way, he was all smiles that day too, and that was good for both of them—a much-needed break from dealing with the illness and associated treatment.

The next day, many of the family members sent Mary energy in a group distance-healing session, as guided by her older sister. At the same time we all sent energy for whatever was in Mary's highest intentions. I sat in our den with Brayden and Briella, who was four years old at the time. We each held one hand up, closed our eyes, and focused on sending energy to her. It definitely helped because I didn't see her for a couple of months.

She was doing well, continuing her treatments and using her Reiki to help balance her own energy regularly.

Then my mother called and said Mary was in the hospital. The doctors were trying a different treatment with her, and she would be there for a couple of days. I drove up with my parents and Briella to visit her. On the way up I stopped and bought a dozen pink roses. Fresh flowers, especially brightly colored ones, could cheer anyone up, plus their energy was high vibration. Mary had an affinity for flowers and plants, so I knew it would make her smile.

As soon as we got into the elevator, I bubbled the energy of Briella and me. I knew there would be a lot of energy in the hospital, and I didn't want to get bombarded by it. Bubbling was a physic shielding visualization technique that I learned early on from my guides, and it's an exercise in my first book, *Discovering the Medium Within*. I just pictured a giant bubble filled with whatever color of energy that made me feel safe. I changed the colors depending on the situation. The bubble would encompass my entire body, and nothing could get in or out of the bubble. It is an effective way of shielding oneself from the energy of others and the environmental energy of places.

We walked into the gray room and saw Mary propped up on pillows, her face smiling, as usual. We all hugged and kissed her. Shamus stood off to the side of the room, smiling and waving to everyone.

"I figured you needed some nature in this room," I said as I handed her the roses.

"They're beautiful," she said, sniffing them gently. When the nurse came in the room, I asked her for a vase or cannister to arrange the flowers. She handed me a plastic green water pitcher. I took the lid off, and Briella and I arranged the flowers. My parents were talking to Mary and Shamus, and I looked out the large picture window. Thick blue-gray clouds blanketed the sky, as though waiting for the perfect moment to shower rain upon everything below. Briella went over to the bed and asked Mary how she was feeling. I saw Mary's face illuminate, and a smile grew across her face as she tried to act like she was feeling great.

"Are you going home today?" Briella asked.

"I should be going soon. I miss my cats," she said.

Shamus stood motionless, like a statue, in the corner. He looked like a shell of a person, and I could see the distance in his eyes—like he needed to step back from all of this and disconnect emotionally. It seemed like he was in a safe place where he couldn't feel anything. I kept the conversation casual with him. We spoke of the cats and the house.

Mary asked for energy, so I sat next to the bed and held her hand. She closed her eyes and rested her head back on the pillow as I placed both my hands on her forearm. She said she could feel the energy in her feet, and I knew she needed grounding. Her mind was filled with worries of finances, her husband, and her cats; last on the list was her own health. My parents conversed with Shamus while I worked on Mary. I knew the energy work made Shamus uncomfortable because he didn't believe in it; Mary had told me so when she came for healing sessions, so my parents were a welcome diversion. After about ten minutes, Mary said she was very tired. We decided to leave so she could get some much-needed rest.

She was in and out of the hospital several times after that first visit. It seemed like every time we thought she was in the clear, another issue would pop up. At one point she had finished the radiation treatments, but they found the cancer had spread to the bones. She had a tremendous fight on her hands, and although I offered to work with her, she often declined because she was too weak and tired. It seemed like her body was breaking down from the treatment or maybe the stress of it all; I couldn't quite tell, but I knew when I spoke with her on the phone that it seemed like she was barely present.

At the same time, we were dealing with the lingering effects of Hurricane Sandy, which had come through like a tidal wave, washing destruction over everything in its path, leaving scattered fragments of lives, like puzzle pieces, all over the state in its wake. It would be a long time before the Jersey Shore was put back together from such a tragedy, but we were Jersey strong and united to help support our communities. In the end we learned that New Jersey was stronger than Hurricane Sandy, and, more importantly, we saw a beautiful side of humanity that's often overlooked in our expedient society. Although it was a good ten to fourteen days before many of us had any power or heat, the dark time was humbling, and I think it made many of us shine our lights brighter. Many of us were softened and transformed by the experience. Our hearts were opened, and we realized how deeply we were connected to everyone around us.

Mary went back in the hospital because she had an infection in her spinal fluid and was in extreme pain. The hospital was running all kinds of tests to determine the exact infection so they could treat it properly. I visited her again, but this time I didn't bring Briella with me. She was sleeping when I walked into the room. Shamus shook her foot and woke her. When Mary opened her eyes, he said, "Anysia's here." She looked to her left and smiled at me. I stepped closer to the bed and patted her arm gently with my fingertips.

"I'm so tired; it must be the medication," she said. I knew they were sedating her to help block out the pain.

"Sleep is good. We could all use some of that," I said. She chuckled a bit, then held her hand out to me, wrapping her fingers tightly around mine. She looked into my eyes and said, "Heal me! I don't want to die," as tears of desperation slid down her cheeks. I felt my eyes well up and my heart pained because I knew I couldn't heal anyone. Everyone had to heal themselves. I was just the conduit for the energy—a helper.

"You're okay. It's gonna be fine," I said, lying right to her face. I felt horrible for lying to her but I couldn't tell her the truth. She was already broken, and I had to give her hope because there was always the possibility that she would heal herself if she did what she needed to do. I couldn't tell her anything that would shatter that reflection of hope. I only visited her for about ten minutes because then she fell asleep again. As soon as I stepped out of her room and into the hallway, my tears flowed and I cried all the way to the elevator. I felt like someone had glued a huge weight to my chest that I couldn't pull off. I knew it was most likely the last conversation I would have with her. On the drive home I sent Mary energy for whatever was in her highest intentions. I also asked some of our passed-on relatives, including her sister Gail, to be with Mary and help guide her in her transition. That night Brayden and I sent energy to Mary from our den, and

I also called my brother Kyle and told him to send her energy for whatever was in her highest intentions. We all sent energy for about twenty minutes that night.

I got another call from my mother a couple of days later. Mary had been moved to a different hospital closer to her home. My mother said that Mary wasn't doing well and we should go and say goodbye. That night we visited her in the hospital again. When we went in the room, Mary wasn't conscious; she was heavily medicated. I sat on a bench next to Brayden at the foot of her bed. I asked Brayden to give her energy. He put his hands up with his palms facing outward and closed his eyes, and I did the same. As soon as the energy flowed, many of the relatives in spirit filed into the room and stood around the bed. Mary's sister, parents, maternal grandmother, and two aunts were there. I knew that they were getting ready to help her transition to the spirit world.

In my mind I told Mary that it was time for her to go and she needed to get ready to leave and just let go. Although physically unconscious, she could still communicate telepathically.

"I know what I need to do. I'm waiting to say my goodbyes," she said. I was surprised by her very self-assured response. I asked her if she needed anything and she said no but thanked me for being there. I told her I loved her and would continue to send her energy over the next few days to ease her transition. I opened my tear-filled eyes and wiped them with a tissue.

"She's leaving, Mommy," Brayden said. I nodded my head and hugged him. We left the room so other family members could go in and visit her.

Two days later we got a call and were told that Mary had passed at the age of fifty-five. I hung up the phone and sobbed for several moments. I told Brayden that Mary had passed. He said that he felt a little sad but knew she wasn't sick and suffering anymore. He gave me a hug and said, "Remember, she's with all those spirits we saw in the hospital." That did make me smile a bit because I knew she was okay.

When we went to the evening viewing for Mary, Briella didn't understand why Mary couldn't talk. Since she was only four years old, she hadn't experienced a funeral. I think it was difficult to wrap her little mind around the fact that she'd seen Mary in the hospital laughing and smiling and now she couldn't talk or smile anymore. I explained that Mary had changed. What we were seeing was Mary's body; her soul—Mary's spirit—had left her broken body and was now living with God in heaven.

"Is it like when a caterpillar leaves the chrysalis and changes to a butterfly? Mary's soul is a butterfly that flew up to God?" she asked, raising her palm gently like she was lifting a tiny butterfly in it. I couldn't have said it better myself. She had just watched the butterfly transition in her preschool a few weeks earlier. They had the chrysalises in the classroom and then observed the transformations to butterflies. I was fascinated that she made the connection between that experience and Mary's transition. Sometimes the youngest children are the oldest souls that teach us magnificent lessons.

"Yes, baby girl. That's exactly what it's like," I said. Her eyes lit up and a smile of accomplishment graced her sweet little face.

Mary's funeral Mass was held the next morning at a Catholic church, where most of our other family funerals were held.

The priest was very young and charismatic. Some of Mary's nieces knew him from when they were in high school. When he approached the pulpit to deliver the homily, Mary appeared, standing right next to him on the right side. I casually looked around to see if anyone else saw her standing there. No one seemed to notice, so I assumed they didn't see her. Ironically, she wasn't wearing the white dress she had on at the funeral parlor. She wore jeans and a blue New York Giants football jersey. In my mind I asked why she had that outfit on.

She said, "This is me. This is what I'd wear to my funeral." To her right side were her older sister Gail and their mother, my Aunt Marie. I was supposed to take note of Aunt Marie's flip-flops that she had on. They were thin, orange, and plastic. She had always worn those kind of flip-flops when she was alive. The three of them were happy and smiling. The priest mentioned that our loved ones in spirit are always helping us. We can talk to them by sending them thoughts and we can always ask them to help us. I was amazed to hear him say this, as I had never really heard a priest speak of this concept in a church setting. I couldn't tell if that was my family inspiring him with those words or if he was just very progressive. Either way, he was the right person to deliver Mary's homily. After the Mass we all gathered outside the church. Many family members were in town from other parts of the country. It's such a strange dichotomy the way death brings everyone together in sadness and love.

The repast was held at Mary's house. We brought trays of food for the grieving family members and friends. I was too sad to cook anything, so I went to Costco and bought a few trays of cookies and brownies. I set them on the kitchen table so Shamus could put them out for everyone. When I walked into Mary's den, I saw the pink quartz I had given her on the glass table next to the television, right where she said she would put it. It made me smile when I saw it there.

I was delighted to connect with my cousins visiting from the South. We spoke in the corner of the kitchen about energy and healing and spirit visits from loved ones. It was good to see them and share in their energy and experiences. I saw Shamus in the kitchen. He was so lost emotionally and his somber eyes conveyed that he was barely hanging on. I felt compassion for him because Mary was an amazing source of love in his life. I wondered how he would live without her there.

A little over a year after Mary's passing, she visited me in spirit. She came with her sister Gail one night as I laid in bed waiting for sleep. They stood at the end of my bed and Mary said that Shamus was going to need help. He was in darkness with his alcoholism, which had progressed rapidly since her passing. She said that he would need help crossing over. I told her that I couldn't help him because I felt he was partly responsible for her being sick and dying. Mary said that this was the way it was supposed to be for the two of them. She spoke about a sacred agreement between them in which she was here to give Shamus unconditional love, as she had by her life and especially by her death. I said that I felt if she would have left him, she would still be here, and I had resentment for him. Mary said that we don't always know what experiences souls need to have in this life. She told me that their souls honored that sacred contract that involved unconditional love and I needed to let go of that resentment and feel love for his healing soul. I said I would work on it. She made me promise to work on it.

"Do everything with love," she told me, and then they were gone. If anyone was meant to teach love, it was Mary because she was totally loving and sweet. I always felt loved by her.

About five months later we got a message that Shamus had passed. They found him in the house, where he had died of intoxication. I shielded my own energy in a bright blue bubble, called in my guides and Archangel Michael, and then I sent light to him. There was so much darkness in that house. I asked the angels to help him cross to where his soul could be healed. I promised Mary I would help, and I couldn't break that promise to her. For the next few nights I sent light to Shamus for whatever was in his soul's highest intentions.

Mary's death was a huge lesson for me in forgiveness and letting go. I had to release the judgments I had for Shamus. I'm certainly not perfect, and I'm not in a position to judge anyone. I'm just a bystander—an observer in all of this—and I needed to remember that fact. I don't know what God and the souls have planned for their growth on this earth. I just need to step aside and allow the process to unfold. I'm here to hold the light and be a loving conduit.

Sometimes healing means letting go. It may not be physical healing or the type of healing we've conjured in our minds. We trust that all experiences are in line with God's healing for that soul. I thanked Mary for teaching me those lessons with loving compassion.

Grounding Your Energy Directly in the Earth

When we think of healing ourselves, we may not recognize that we can use the energy of the earth, which is all around us, if we are attuned to it. We might include our focused intentions. We may also include any prayers or invocations of assistance to loved ones in the spirit world, masters of light, saints, and spiritual deities. Sometimes the energy most readily available to us is often overlooked.

I went for a run with Brayden, who was riding his BMX bike alongside me. Through the thick, humid air, we made our way to the newly extended bike path, which was lightly covered in gravel bits, as it had yet to be paved. Mounded heaps of sandy soil lined the path. Brayden proceeded to jump these heaps on his bike in a zigzag pattern. At one point the bike slipped out from under him—in an instant he was on the ground, with the bike handlebar pressed into his badly scraped chest that was bleeding right through his shirt. Gasping for air, he chanted, "Mom, please give me energy. Please give me energy." His big brown eyes glossed. I knelt down and placed my palms on his legs. I told him to calm his energy and heal himself. I felt his energy settle as the vibration flowed from my palms, but I also noticed a buzzing sensation from the ground.

As I held my palms against him, my eyes scanned the sandy ground. Tiny quartz crystals reflected the sun's light all around us. I hadn't noticed them when we got on the path, but at eye level it was blatantly visible and the ground's energy pulsed vibrantly. The little crystals reminded me of the kind found in Cape May, a little seashore Victorian retreat located at the southernmost tip of New Jersey and favorite vacation place of mine for its amazing energy. Cape May has an abundance of natural jasper forms in its soil, but it also has tiny quartz crystals in the sand, also known as Cape May diamonds.

Brayden felt it, too. Although he didn't know why, he said the sand made him feel calm and relaxed. I picked up a few of the crystals and showed him how the sand was filled with them.

"This sand has very high vibrational healing energy," I said. I thought about taking a few of the crystals home and placing them around the yard, but then I realized they were there for a reason and might help someone else down the road. I silently thanked the universe for providing these amplified healing tools. About five minutes later, Brayden rose to his feet and mounted his bike. Although still sore, he felt well enough to continue to ride for another two miles.

The earth exudes its own healing energy from the ground. It extends upward through all things connected to it—trees, grass, sand, and all plants. The energy is always available to help us heal; we just need to step outside and connect with it. We are given all the tools we need in this life. It is just a matter of tuning in and using them.

> *What you will need for this exercise:* access to grass,
> sand, or dirt—your bare feet need direct contact
> with the earth
>
> • • • •
>
> Walk outside barefoot on grass, sand, or dirt.
> Walk in a large circle three or four times.
>
> As your feet connect to the ground, physically
> feel it and note the way the sand, dirt, or grass feels,

as well as any emotions that come up as you connect to the ground.

Stand in one spot and envision all the energy flowing down from your head, down your neck, and into your chest. As it reaches your chest and grounds your heart and lungs, it feels solid. It moves down to the abdomen, through the hips, and into your thighs. From your thighs, you feel it flow into your calves and down to your ankles. From your ankles, it moves into your feet.

As the energy connects from your feet to the earth, you feel solid, like a tree deeply rooted in the ground. Stand straight up and allow yourself to embrace this solidity. Allow the earth's magnetic current to anchor within you.

You are deeply connected and united with the earth. You are centered and peaceful. Say these words to yourself a few times as you relish this special connection.

Know that you can use this exercise to center yourself anytime you feel overwhelmed, scattered, or disconnected.

• • • •

5

Alzheimer's and Dementia

I wanted to volunteer at a care facility or hospice organization. I thought it would be a good way to give back to the community and help people. At that time most care facilities were not very familiar with energy healing, but I found a holistic hospice organization that administered all types of alternative therapies, such as aromatherapy, massage, Reiki, and acupressure, to hospice patients as well as their caretakers. It seemed like the right organization, so I enrolled in the volunteer training program.

After a few brief training sessions, I was approved to administer healing sessions to patients. My first assignment entailed giving a healing session to a woman in a long-term care facility a few minutes from my home. She was in the final stages of Alzheimer's and had been classified as "failure to thrive" by the medical staff. I was excited and a little nervous because it was my first encounter giving energy to an Alzheimer's patient, and I didn't know what to expect. I had heard that they could become agitated and sometimes combative. I hoped to avoid any experience like that with the client.

I parked my car and stared momentarily at the large brown brick-face building as nervousness knitted my stomach into a blanket of nausea. In my mind I called out to my maternal grandmother, Nanny. Nanny had been an activity director at a nursing home in Alexandria, Virginia. She worked with all types of geriatric patients while exhibiting tremendous compassion and patience. She suffered a severe stroke right after my undergraduate college graduation and died two weeks later. A constant source of love for me, Nanny became my buddy when I went to school in Baltimore, Maryland, and she lived in Arlington, Virginia. I visited every other weekend and she taught me to sew, garden, and cook some of her favorite Italian recipes.

I was always deeply connected to her. After she died, Nanny was one of the people who helped me accept my abilities, and she assisted me in my first crossing over of a spirit. She was a teacher for me in her life and also through her physical death. I knew I needed her guidance because she had experience with Alzheimer's and dementia.

I asked her to be with me at the care facility and to help out if needed. I always called to her when I needed help with anything or if I just wanted to feel loved. I felt her warm energy pulsating to my left side and an overwhelming sense of love enveloped me. It touched my heart, and a few tears slipped out of my eyes. I thanked her for being there with me. I knew she was there to ease any fears I had with this new experience.

The building had a peculiar energy. As I entered through the doors, I felt a heaviness, like an invisible cement ceiling, hanging above the place, blocking everything below it. The inside was tidy and clean, with lots of lights, but the weighted energy stifled me. I approached the peach-colored counter at the nurses' station and introduced myself and explained that I was there to give healing energy to a patient. I politely asked the three nurses behind the counter to direct me to the patient's room. The nurse on the end smirked while she rolled her eyes and pushed a mini powdered doughnut into her mouth. The brown-haired nurse to the right smiled pleasantly, came around the counter, and greeted me. She had soft hazel eyes that matched her gentle energy. She told me her name was Denise and then escorted me to room 205. She informed me that the patient could not speak or move and had been in that state for more than four months.

I stepped through the door and noticed the pale, frail woman with white hair reclining in the bed. Her door displayed her name: Frances. The pale yellow–colored room was very clean and filled with lots of family pictures. It held a light scent of flowery shampoo.

Though she couldn't speak to me, I introduced myself to Frances and explained a bit about the energy work I was about to do with her. I felt the need to tell her everything I was doing because I believed she could hear and understand me. I said a brief prayer to shield us and the space and to center myself. As soon as I placed my hands above her head, I heard her say telepathically that she felt trapped. Since I had no experience with her condition, I didn't really understand what she meant.

I continued to work on her head, and as the energy transferred from my hands to Frances, it grew stronger and felt like she had a magnet at the top of her head drawing all the energy into her. Then I heard Nanny say that with Alzheimer's and dementia patients there was a spirit/body disconnect. The spirit knew it was time to leave, but the connection between the body and spirit was broken, so the body lingered. I asked her how she knew this, and she said it was part of her job on the other side. Nanny explained that she would be called to help these patients because they did not always leave when they needed to cross over.

Physical death is a continuation of the life process. The soul leaves the material body behind and moves into the spirit realm. Everyone continues to grow and evolve on the other side. Many people believe that as soon as you leave your physical body, you automatically ascend to the level of a highly advanced soul like Mother Teresa. This is not the case. Whatever ascension level someone is at during the time of physical death in this life that is where they continue on the other side. There, the soul will be assigned a job and continue the learning and evolutionary process. Soul work on the other side may include working with humans on the earth plane, working with spirit guides, or working with spirits in the spirit realm or somewhere in between. Nanny's job was to work with the spirit guides of primarily elderly people with broken body/spirit connections. She would help them cross over from the physical world to the spirit world. Her job in human life had prepared her for working with that population in her spirit life. She had spent over twenty years working in a nursing facility with geriatric patients. I was grateful to have her assistance with Frances, and I thanked her for being by my side in spirit, just as she had done in her physical life.

I continued with the session. At one point Frances tilted her head, looked directly into my eyes, and smiled happily at me. This puzzled me because the nurse had said that Frances couldn't move. I wondered if they were wrong about her condition—if there was some mistake. I smiled back at her and finished up the session by grounding her energy down to her feet. She seemed peaceful. I hoped Frances would sleep well that night, and I told her that I would see her again the following week.

About an hour after I left the care facility, I was in my kitchen making some chamomile tea when a strong flowery smell wafted by me. Within a few seconds the smell engulfed the entire room. I didn't have any flowers in the house at the time, and I began to sniff my own clothes to see if the fragrance was coming from me. Although it wasn't generated from me, the scent was all around me, yet I couldn't identify its source. It smelled familiar—and then I recognized it. Having smelled it shortly before returning home, I identified it as the flowery shampoo smell from Frances's room, but I wasn't sure why it was in my home. I went upstairs and took a shower, thinking I might have picked up the smell from working with her. Perhaps it was on my skin or in my clothing in some way. When I came back downstairs, the smell had dissipated.

The following week I went back to the nursing facility for another session with Frances. Since I knew where I was going and had already signed in at the front desk, I didn't need to stop at the nurses' station. But when I went into room 205, there was a different patient in the bed—an elderly man. I quickly exited and headed down the hall to the nurses' station. Nurse Denise was behind the counter again. When I inquired about Frances's whereabouts, she informed me that Frances had passed on. I asked when it had happened because the hospice coordinator had not informed me of a change in assignment.

"It was about a half hour after you left last week," she said. I bit down on my lower lip, pondering the circumstances. I thought I was supposed to help her. How could she die right after I left? Nurse Denise studied my face and then said kindly, "She went peacefully in her sleep." I smiled and thanked her for her time. She was an angelic light, and her soft energy contrasted sharply against the heaviness of the place. As I walked to the front door, I realized that I *had* helped Frances. I had been called there to help Frances leave her body behind. She had been trapped in that state for several months. I also understood that Nanny had been there to aid in the transition as well. The flowery shampoo smell in my house was Frances's way of thanking me as she moved on.

As I drove away from the hospital, I thanked Frances for allowing me to help her cross over, and I also thanked Nanny for aiding me in the process. Our loved ones who experience dementia or dementia-related illnesses on earth are free of these ailments when they pass on. Sometimes they need a little help getting across, but once there, they enter the spirit world without any of those limitations that bound them to the earth plane.

EXERCISE

Walking in Grace

Many times in our lives, we seek to control our experiences involving ourselves, other people, and situations. But often we have very little control. We're always in control of our own energy and our responses to experiences, but everything else is out of our hands. Surrendering to this fact can be difficult because it means letting go of the ego. But when we let go and surrender to the Divine, we can walk in grace knowing all our initiatives are supported for whatever is in our highest intentions. Things will work out as they should for whatever is best for our souls.

The term *grace* has a variety of definitions based on the context in which it's used. For this exercise we will go with the definition of moving through something with ease and serenity. When we talk about grace in this capacity, we're referring to that which comes from surrendering to the divine process. When we kick the ego to the curb and follow our soul's intuition, we allow the divine source to flow into our lives and take us on the path that's best suited for our souls. We'll experience all that is necessary and meet all the right people who will help our souls evolve.

Getting to this point of surrendering and letting go takes some work on our part. The ego is earthbound and relegated to the physical body and mind, but the soul is different; the soul is the essence of our true selves. It's an eternal and unconditionally loving part of the divine source. When we shed the ego like an orange peel, what's revealed underneath is sweet, beautiful, and amazing—pure golden goodness. The soul is a reflection of divine love, so the more we move into the vibration of unconditional love, the more we connect to the Divine. This deep connection to the Divine is what bestows grace upon us. When we let go and surrender, we're connected to the source and completely aligned with our soul purpose. As we walk in grace, we're constantly supported on our journey and can trust that we're on the right path. Let go, surrender, and walk in grace!

What you will need for this exercise: a place to walk
outdoors; it is best to walk in a park or on a
wooded path—someplace where you can both
concentrate and connect with nature

• • • •

Take your shoes off and connect your feet to the
earth.

Begin walking and let your thoughts flow
through your mind. Just let whatever thoughts
come up and let them release. Allow this process
of letting things surface mentally and then releasing them go on for a few minutes. Don't follow the
thoughts. Let them go!

As you walk, take note of all the sights and
sounds you encounter in your environment. Listen
to the birds, perhaps you hear them chirping. See
them flying in and out of the trees. Maybe you will
see a few squirrels gathering nuts and flicking their
tails as they scurry along the ground. Spend a few
moments focusing and really tuning in to the sights
and sounds of the walk.

Now, tune out all the sounds and sights and continue walking along the path. Tune in to the divine
energy. For a few minutes think of all the things you
are trying to control in your life—all the things you
are creating resistance to and are feeling stressed or
tired about. Using your mind, say to the Divine that
you are letting go of the illusion of control over all
of these things, releasing all resistance. State that
you completely surrender to the process for what-

ever is in your highest good. Consciously choose to let go and feel all obstructions being pulled from upward through all your chakras and exiting through the crown chakra, at the top of the head. Then feel everything clearing through the auric layers that surround the physical body.

Keep walking at a pace that suits you and feel the connection between your crown chakra and the source above you. Your head might feel a little flighty or you might feel like stuff is moving around above your head. This is your connection to what will be guiding you.

As you walk, use your mind and ask the Divine what you can do to surrender more deeply to the process unfolding before your soul. How can you let go more? Make a mental note of any guidance or instruction you receive. You may hear information, you may see images, or you may feel it. The information will come through whichever psychic sense is strongest for you.

Thank the Divine for walking with you and helping you let go and surrender to all opposition.

You can do this exercise anytime you feel blocked or when you feel like things aren't flowing smoothly in your life. Walk with the Divine and gracefully surrender to the process.

•   •   •   •

6

Animals Helping Us Heal

Animals help us heal in amazing ways, though we don't always recognize it.

Simon, aka Simie, was an active eleven-year-old yellow Labrador retriever who lived with my parents, but my youngest brother, Kyle, had a special affinity for him and would sometimes dognap him for days and take him to his condo for "bro time." My mother would come home to an empty house and then call all her children trying to locate her prized four-legged son.

He was a man's dog, voraciously licking his private parts on display in the center of the den whenever my parents had a house full of guests. He would playfully jump on the lap of anyone sitting on the couch, bearing down all his weight while panting his jellyfish-scented breath in their faces. I always felt that he would have been a great fraternity house dog.

Once we were at the ocean with our female chocolate Labrador at the time, Princess. She was resting calmly on a blanket, enjoying the sun. My parents showed up with Simon, and he spotted Princess and came rushing over to her. My dad was holding Simon by the leash, but Simon pulled my dad across the sand as if he were on skis. Simon got right next to Princess's blanket and immediately rolled his whole body in the sand and then dug a shallow hole and set himself in it, panting wildly like he had just run a long-distance race. I think he was trying to be her friend, but Princess remained unmoved and looked away from him, as though repulsed by the sandy mess he had created for himself. She ignored him the entire day and any time he tried to get close to her, she gave a little growl and he immediately stepped back.

Despite his slightly uncouth behavior, Simon's lovable nature made him irresistible. He was all about having fun. Sometimes when my brothers played with him, he would get really excited and scrunch up his nose and grit his teeth as though he were smiling. They'd joke and say, "Oh boy, this guy's smiling; he's feelin' good," which would only excite him more. What you saw was what you got with Simon; no frills, just love and lots of goofiness. He was a sweet boy who didn't have a mean bone in his body. I don't think I ever once heard him growl at anyone.

My parents had acquired him accidentally. An attendant at a gas station close to their house was getting rid of his two-year-old dog because the dog was getting very big and the man could not take care of him. The man worked long hours and rented a house that lacked a fenced-in yard, so he walked the dog before and after work, but the rest of the day the dog spent in a cage. My mother's neighbor, an avid dog lover, was always looking to help out a dog in need. She knew that my parents had lost their dog a year earlier and told my parents about the gas station attendant's situation.

My dad went to the man's house to look at Simon. When he arrived at the house, the eighty-plus-pound dog was in his cage, where he could barely move. The man opened the cage and Simon ran around the house from room to room like a pinball bouncing off the inside of the game. My dad said he kept turning his head and watching the man chase Simon with the leash. Eventually the man caught up with Simon and secured the leash around his neck.

He led Simon to the backyard, and my dad said the dog was jumping four feet in the air, straight up and down, like a pogo stick.

"Well, he's got some strong legs," my dad said to Simon's owner. The man chuckled and asked my father if he wanted the dog. My dad said that the dog was nice, but he needed to make sure that he was good with children because he watched my son a couple of days a week. My father asked if he could come back with his grandson. The man said he could come back later that night.

Around 5:00 p.m. my dad drove by my house and we followed his car. Simon's house was just two blocks from mine. The man brought the dog over to us, and once again Simon was so excited that he was jumping straight up and down repeatedly. Brayden giggled and petting him on the back every time Simon landed. He was such a friendly dog and had so much love to give. He jumped up and licked all of us on the face. He just wanted to play and have fun.

"Well, he's definitely friendly," I noted.

"Whaddaya think, Brayden? Should I keep him?" my father asked.

"Yeah, Papa. He's cool!" Brayden said, giving my dad a thumb's-up sign with his little hand. My dad nodded to Simon's owner.

"We'll take him," my father said, and within twenty minutes Simon's life changed dramatically. Then the man handed the leash to my younger brother, Kyle. He took the leash and started running with Simon down the street. The two were already connected. They ran at the same pace, and both of them looked so happy on the run back toward us.

My father asked the man if he was from Newark because he had a distinct accent. My father was a retired deputy chief of thirty-two years in the city of Newark, New Jersey. The man said that he was from Newark—north Newark actually, which was part of my father's district that he covered. Then my father asked what street the man had lived on, and he said that he lived on Stone Street. My father knew the street well because there had been a big fire there during his tour, where there was an infant trapped in the dwelling. The man said he had lived in building 75. My father knew the three-story brick building, which was a six family multi-dwelling. That was the building where they had the big fire.

"Were you there during the fire?" my father asked.

"Yes, I showed the chief the back entrance to get into the building," the man said.

"That was me! I was the first one on the scene, and I called the rescue squad," my father said. Although the Newark Fire Department rescue squad was able to save the baby from the burning building, the baby later died from complications at the hospital. The two men recalled the details of the tragic fire and discussed the coincidental connection they shared.

My father drove Simon to his new home. When we got to my parents' house, my father opened the back gate and they walked through the yard. He let Simon off the leash, and the dog ran around the yard as fast as he could. He was sprinting around the pool as if it were a mini racetrack. It was so funny because the dog looked like he was smiling. He ran around for a good ten minutes. He stopped for a few seconds to get some fresh water from a bowl my mom had placed in the yard for him, and then he ran some more. He tired himself out a bit, and then he came in the house and my mother fed him in his new bowl. She loved him immediately and talked to him in a baby voice like she was talking to a young child. He looked up at her and I could see the bond between them. Simon finally had a mommy who would love and snuggle him. He had left a cage life and been adopted into a kingdom where he was a prince and would have two people showering him with bonies, toys, and lots of love. He didn't know it yet, but he had just hit the lottery *big time*!

Initially, Simon carried a bit of anxiety in his energy. Brayden and I placed our hands on his back to settle his energy. I think he had developed the anxiety from always being caged. He had a lot of energy because he was young and being caged up, that energy had nowhere to go, so it just vibrated in him. After a few months at my parents' house, he settled down. He had a big house, a yard to run in, and basically every dog toy imaginable. My mother loved him because he was very affectionate and soaked up her attention.

Simon had a deep connection to Kyle, my younger brother, who worked as a bartender and would come home in the early hours of the morning. Simon would lay on the Oriental run in the downstairs foyer by the front door, waiting patiently for Kyle. Upon Kyle's return, the two would sit together and watch TV until Kyle unwound, and then they'd head up to bed and sleep most of the day.

When Kyle moved into a condo with his girlfriend, he still came home once a week to spend time with Simon. Sometimes he dognapped him and took him to his condo for a bro-time sleepover. There, they'd order a pizza and stay up and watch TV or Kyle would play video games while Simon hung out on the bed with him. The two were buddies and there was a lot of brotherly love between them.

Simon had always been healthy and loved going to the veterinarian. All the people in the vet office loved him because he was so upbeat and friendly. I wonder if he liked going there because he associated it with treats because he never had any real health ailments until Kyle got sick.

When Kyle started his cancer treatment, Simon knew something was wrong. His energy changed. He was by Kyle constantly like he was guarding him. Whenever Kyle came home from his chemotherapy treatments, he would be sick in bed for about a week and Simon would stay in his room and sleep at the foot of his bed until Kyle regained his strength and was well enough to assume his normal routine.

After Kyle's second round of treatment, he called me over to give him energy. When I entered the cave-like room, cold and dimly lit with curtains drawn, I saw Simon at the foot of the bed.

Kyle lay there weak and tired, barely able to raise his head from the nausea. Simon slept with his eyes closed and didn't even open them to make eye contact with me. The dog looked like he was praying or concentrating because his eyes were sealed shut. This was the dog that always jumped on everyone and licked their faces as they entered the house. It seemed like he could feel Kyle's cancer. Simon seemed sick and sad at the same time; I couldn't figure it out. As I worked on Kyle and moved from his head to his feet, Simon remained motionless with his eyes closed. I asked my brother about it and he said that this is what Simon did whenever he came home from treatment. It was quite normal for Simon, apparently.

Throughout all four rounds of chemotherapy, the dog remained by Kyle's side. After his rounds of treatment, Kyle endured a lymph node removal surgery, in which the doctors extracted eighty-two lymph nodes from his groin area up through to his lungs. The recovery was painful, and Kyle couldn't eat solids. He spent almost seven days in the hospital. When he returned, Simon was once again next to his bed until his master recovered.

A few months after Kyle's surgery, I had a premonition that he would have cancer again in March of the following year. Although he had beaten it physically, he was still working on the root of why he had manifested the illness. This was an ongoing process for him as he grew in love and acceptance for himself. Kyle had a feeling that he would get cancer again, too. He relayed that to me and often stressed about it. Though his scans and bloodwork came back clean each month, he could not shake the feeling that the cancer was stalking him. I kept the premonition to myself because I didn't want to scare him, plus I wasn't sure if it was a fear-based projection since I was so close to my little brother.

I had a little anxiety as I turned my calendar page from February to March that year. I waited patiently for Kyle to get his monthly cancer scans at Memorial Sloan Kettering in New York City. Kyle's scans came back clean, but Simon was not so lucky.

My mother noticed a large cyst growing in Simon's hind area. She took him to the veterinarian for testing. After a barrage of tests, my parents found out that Simon had advanced anal gland cancer. The doctors offered my parents a couple of different options. They could do nothing and just keep him comfortable or they could give him a chemotherapy pill. Like all chemotherapy treatments, the canine version had side effects. It could make him nauseous and tired. Plus, his bowel movements needed to be picked up immediately and the grass had to be washed with soap and water because of the chemicals passing through his body.

My parents couldn't understand how Simon had seen the vet four months earlier for his annual exam and bloodwork and there were no signs of the disease, yet now he had a golf ball–sized malignant tumor in his groin. The veterinarian didn't have a logical explanation for the disease. It was declared idiopathic because there was no real understanding of why he had manifested it. Our explanation is that the dog had, in fact, absorbed the disease so my brother could live longer on the earth.

As soon as I heard the news of Simon's illness, I called Kyle. He was very emotional about it and knew that the dog had taken the illness on for him. We discussed ways to keep Simon comfortable, which included weekly energy-healing treatments.

Kyle, who was now a Reiki Master, agreed to give Simon weekly healing sessions. He said it was the least he could do to repay Simon for such a compassionate act. I witnessed a session in which Simon rested comfortably as Kyle gently swept his hands across Simon's massive chest, his breaths deep and relaxed.

I would also give Simon energy when I visited my parents a couple of times a week. As I worked on him, I knew he wouldn't heal himself and that this was some type of soul agreement he had made to give my brother more time in the physical world. Over the next year, Simon received his chemo pill but the cancer grew and the tumor evolved into something larger than a baseball. Simon had difficulty passing his bowel movements and was eating less. He seemed less energetic, and we knew the ending was near. My mother had prayed for a sign so that she would know when the time was right if she was called to put him down. It was a difficult dichotomy because although the cancer grew, Simon was of sound mind and stayed actively involved with the family.

Then I got a call early in the morning from my dad. He asked me to come over and give Simon energy because the dog had had a seizure and couldn't move. They wanted to get him up and into the car so they could take him to the vet. I said I would come over right after I got Brayden on the school bus.

Apparently, Simon had been totally fine and then he just started seizing on the floor for about ten to fifteen minutes. My mother comforted him as his body shook uncontrollably. When the seizing stopped, his body was stiff for a few minutes, though he could move his eyes. My parents kept talking to him and petting him. Kyle had stopped by that morning to check on

Simon, so he had been there the whole time during the seizure and had lain right next to his old pal and hugged him. Kyle was there for Simon the same way Simon had been there for Kyle. Soon Simon began wagging his tail and he was able to move his limbs. Then he sat up and panted with his mouth wide open, as if he were smiling.

My parents took Simon to the vet right after he recovered from the seizure. Of course, they knew it was time because Simon's condition had progressed rapidly, despite the chemotherapy medication and everything else they were doing to keep him comfortable. My parents felt they were doing the right thing by putting him to sleep because although his mind worked great, his body was failing him and he was in pain. After just under a year of battling cancer, Simon passed.

The bonds between humans and our companion animals are strong and sometimes these compassionate animals do something extraordinary: they absorb the illnesses of their humans, so their owners do not have to experience the physical suffering or so that their humans can spend more time on the earth.

Our pets are selfless companions who sometimes make the ultimate sacrifice for us. We can learn the deepest sense of compassion from them. Maybe God created them so we can learn how to be selfless. One thing is for sure: they make our lives comfortable. They brighten our days, comfort us when we're lonely, and warm our hearts. Pets are pure love, and we should be grateful for them because they give so much more than they take in life; they teach us lessons of unconditional love.

Embracing the Vibration
of Unconditional Love in Our Lives

I choose to surround myself in the vibrational energy of unconditional love at all times. Living in this vibration does not negate the existence of evil and lower vibrational energy. I acknowledge the existence of dark energy, but I don't associate with it, nor do I choose to manifest it in my reality.

The vibrations of love are aligned with the Divine and therefore exist at an elevated energetic level. If we acknowledge that all living things are comprised of energy, and energy vibrates and oscillates, then we could also say that different things are vibrating at different rates: the higher the frequency, the faster the rate of energetic vibration. Most evolved spirits, for example, vibrate at a higher rate than humans, which is one of the reasons why seeing spirits can be intangible for many humans: the lower the frequency, the slower the rate of vibration. Therefore, there's a distinct difference between the frequencies of higher and lower vibrational energies.

When we put our intentions out into the universe, we're applying energy to our thoughts. Our thoughts become our words and actions as the universe brings our desired reality to fruition. As a result, we have the potential to manifest whatever we intend. So, we're creating our own realities based on our intentions. Everyone is born to this magnificent earth as a pure soul. Each beautiful child develops into an adult as a culmination of their own thoughts and experiences in this life. People who are manipulative think about ways to manipulate other people and situations. Their thoughts are consumed with manipulation.

They attract other manipulative people who vibrate at the same frequency—hence, they have manifested a reality full of manipulative energy. Angry people obsess over thoughts that fuel anger. Their actions carry anger. They attract other angry people who vibrate at the same frequency, so their realities are full of anger because this is what they have chosen to manifest.

I choose love. My thoughts are full of love. I monitor them to keep them bright. If I find a thought that isn't aligned, I change it. I attract other people who live in the energy of love. This is my reality; I am love, and I choose to be with other loving vibrations. We are given free will to choose light or darkness for ourselves. Which do you choose? Take a step back and look at your world! What have you created for yourself? Is it a brilliant portrait with bright colors and soft lines that gently blend into each other or is it a grayscale photo with sharp, jagged edges boxing you in? If you don't like what you see, change the image! It all begins with your thoughts. Choose to live in the vibration of love.

> *What you will need for this visualization exercise:* a quiet place to relax
>
> • • • •
>
> Sit in a naturally relaxing position for your body. You can lie flat or sit up in a chair.
>
> Once you are in a comfortable position, focus on your breathing. Breathe in peaceful serenity, and breathe out any conflict or stress. Feel all your muscles relax deeper with each breath.
>
> Now that you are in a comfortable position and relaxed, envision a golden ray of light coming from

above you. As it gets closer to you, feel the warmth emanating from it. See this golden light descending and allow it to cascade down from your head to your feet. Feel the warm comfort it brings as it encases your entire being in golden light, shielding you and protecting you from anything other than the vibration of love. Know that you are safe and totally secure wrapped in this golden blanket of protection.

Now that your body and mind are one and you are protected in golden light, you are ready to balance your heart chakra and connect it to the vibration of unconditional love.

Close your eyes, and picture yourself walking through a lush garden filled with beautiful pink blossoms. As you stroll along, feel the smooth stone path under your bare feet and notice the sea of colorful blooms that brightens both sides of your path; a bouquet of sweet flowery scents fills your nose. The afternoon sunshine warms your skin as you think of how totally relaxed you feel. The sea of pink blossoms goes on for miles and the path seems like you could walk it for an eternity, watching the blossom heads rhythmically dancing from side to side as the wind conducts the tempo for them. You see a white wooden bench ahead of you, and you decide to walk toward it and take a seat.

As you sit down, your mind is filled with images and memories of when you experienced unconditional love. Perhaps you recall holding your child for the first time; being hugged by a loved one or embraced by a nurturing friend; or holding a tiny kitten, puppy, or other loving pet for the first time. You sense your deep connection with the Divine as you recall these memories, and you're filled with the loving emotions attached to them.

You sit for a moment and allow yourself to fill with this vibration of unconditional love. You feel it emanating from your heart chakra and pulsating softly in the center of your chest. Place your palm over this area and sense this circular motion. Allow this energy to spread to all the cells in your body until you are overflowing with this beautiful loving vibration.

You stand up, leave the bench, and walk over to the garden in front of you filled with bright pink blossoms. As your feet reach the garden, something is glistening right in front of you. You bend down and kneel on your knees to take a closer look.

As you extend your hand, you feel a piece of stone or some hard object sticking up from the earth. You push away the dirt with your fingertips and unearth a three-inch rounded piece of rose quartz that fits perfectly in the palm of your hand. Hold it in your left palm, which is closest to your heart, and feel the vibration of unconditional love shifting through your entire being.

You look up and notice, between the stems of all the pink blossoms, that there are pieces of rose quartz throughout the garden, hidden in the soil with just snippets poking out at the top, catching the sun's light and casting pink sparkles all over the garden. Place your right hand on the garden soil and connect deeper to the energy of love growing here.

Once you feel the loving vibrations flowing in you and have allowed it to balance your energy, step away from the garden and back onto the path. Keeping the piece of rose quartz in your left hand, begin walking once again down the stone walkway. As you walk, take note of the cardinals and sparrows flying through the air. See the butterflies of all colors sipping nectar from the centers of the colorful blossoms as they flutter their wings in a peaceful cadence. Know that you can return to this garden of love anytime you need to feel loved unconditionally or you feel the need to love yourself deeper.

Now it is time to return to your home. Picture a bright red cord extending from your root chakra, at the base of your spine, way down to the center of the earth's core. Feel the magnetic current pulling all your energy down deeply from your head. It flows down through your head and into your neck. Feel the energy pulled down to the lungs and through the digestive tract. As the energy flows down to the root chakra, the pull is strong. The energy continues down your legs and through your feet. As it reaches your feet, you feel very heavy. You are deeply connected to the earth. You are grounded in the earth's energy and fully present. Sit for a moment and really savor the strength of this connection as it roots you in your life. Now you can release the cord connecting your root chakra to the earth's core. See it falling to the center of the earth and watch it being absorbed into the earth's center. When you are ready, open your eyes, breathe deeply, and know that you are always loved in this life.

. . . .

7

A Voice for the Voiceless

I wanted to experience healing work with animals other than my pets, so I volunteered at the Associated Humane Society's Tinton Falls location. At the time I was an adjunct English professor at the community college a few miles from the shelter. I taught my classes in the morning and headed over to the shelter from 11:30 a.m. to 2:00 p.m. every Tuesday and Thursday. The hours were very specific because I had to be home by 3:00 each day to get Brayden off the school bus. I would balance and give energy to the animals and would also psychically scan some of them, if needed.

I followed a routine each week. I visited the critical care unit first, with the animals who were very sick or recovering from surgery. I gave energy to every animal in each cage. Then I stopped in the free-roam cat room, a large open space where the cats could walk around and climb on things rather than sit in cages all day. Cats love energy, and as soon as I opened the door they all ran over to me and brushed up against my legs. Some purred and others entwined their tails around me. I had a hard time choosing which one to work on first; I have to be honest, I had a couple of favorites. I placed my hands on each cat for a few minutes just to balance them, and then I watched as their bodies relaxed one muscle at a time until they curled up into tiny fur balls. By the time I left the room, all of the cats were snuggled in their beds, sleeping comfortably.

My next stop was the small animal room, which housed ferrets, rabbits, and sometimes reptiles. I held the rabbits on my lap while I worked with them. I had an affinity for rabbits since my first pet was a little gray German Dwarf bunny named November. My undergraduate college roommate and I got her in the fall of our senior year, hence the name November. I don't really remember why we went into the pet shop on York Road in Baltimore, but when we got in there, the little gray and brown bunnies were hopping around in an open pen.

"We're gettin' one of these. They don't make any noise and they're *awesome*," I said to my roommate as I high-fived her. She agreed, and we picked out a solid gray female bunny, some rabbit pellets, a litter pan, and a small bag of cat litter.

No one in the administration ever found out about our furry illegal alien, and we finished the year with our six-inch buddy nestled in our room.

After we graduated, November stayed with me. I took her everywhere I went. I had a big Fendi shopping tote bag with a leather drawstring closure. She traveled cross-country with me, from New Jersey to California, and lived in more states than some humans, including Maryland, Idaho, California, Pennsylvania, and New Jersey.

One day while Brayden was watching cartoons, he noticed something odd about November. He came upstairs and said something was wrong with her. I ran downstairs and saw she was having difficulty breathing. As soon as we took her out of the cage, her breathing labored deeper, and within a few seconds her little heart gave out. She died while Brayden and I were holding her in our hands. We gave her a little bit of energy before she took her last breath, but we couldn't do much more than that to help her.

Brayden was just five years old, but there he was giving healing energy to his bunny in her last moments of life. She lived a great, active fifteen years—clearly better than most house rabbits, as she had exceeded her life expectancy by three years. Whenever I worked with the rabbits at the shelter, fond memories of November hopped through my mind.

Honestly, I wasn't a fan of the shelter ferrets. Sometimes the workers took them out of the cages and let them run around on the floor after it had been mopped. I was afraid the ferrets would bite me. Although they weren't known for being vicious, they moved really quickly with their long, skinny bodies and had ridiculously sharp teeth for such little animals. I never got bit but I always kept a healthy distance and only worked on them when they were in cages.

I walked through the kennel rooms, too, and gave energy to all the dogs in there. The shelter had two kennel rooms, which were lined on both sides with cages of dogs to be adopted. Each cage had an indoor section with a bed and feeding area and then a doggie door that led to an outside covered patio area, where the dogs could relax, get some fresh air, and stretch out. I always felt the office staff and shelter workers embodied tremendous patience and huge hearts because they cared for these homeless animals day in and day out. It took a special kind of person to work in that type of environment—to give hope to the hopeless.

While I worked on a cat that was sitting with the receptionist in the front office, a middle-aged, darkhaired man came in with a twelve-year-old golden retriever. He said he had to turn the dog in because he couldn't keep it anymore. I knew the man was lying by the way he broke eye contact with the worker and stared at the floor. You didn't have to be psychic to see through that lie. The office worker had him fill out paperwork. She explained that it would be hard for the dog to be adopted at that age and it might not find a home. The man said there was nothing he could do. The dog was happy and wagging its tail, clearly unaware of its fate. The worker took the dog and noted that they would have to feature the dog in the *Humane News*, the society's magazine, to let people know about it and give it a better chance at getting adopted at such an old age. She said that she had to go outside and have a cigarette to destress from the heartless man and the possible fate of the sweet dog. I admired the courage of the workers because they dealt with life and death dilemmas involving the animals daily and they didn't let it break their spirits. They kept fighting to place the animals in good homes; it was a true sense of altruism.

After I worked with a few of the kennel dogs, an office worker brought me a small cat from the critical care unit that had been named Itty Bitty Boo by the staff. The little gray cat had several jagged patches of skin and fur missing from her neck. They didn't know what had happened to her, but she had been found walking alone on a street. They asked if I thought she had been hit by a car and maybe dragged. I cupped both hands gently around her small body as the worker held her. I could tell by the way she cowered her head and looked away from me that her spirit had been broken.

When the worker handed her to me, I didn't feel physical pain in her, but the veterinarian had her on a pain medication. As soon as I held her, I felt tremendous sadness that brought me to the point of tears. I placed one hand on top of her little head. The energy flowed immediately, and she absorbed it like a giant sponge. I got some images of a man holding her and cutting her fur off with a razor blade. He was basically skinning her alive. I viewed the trauma of the experience that was imprinted in her energy. Then I saw another image of him opening his apartment door, and I felt her overwhelming fear as she snuck out the door behind him, unnoticed. The frail cat had clearly been tortured, and I tried to give her as much love and healing as possible in my time with her. I told the worker what I had seen. She said she was surprised that a person would be so cruel. I also noted that I saw the man had other cats in the apartment. He was a very sick person and a blatant animal abuser.

The shelter veterinarian continued to treat the cat, but I felt her will to live was weak since she had been traumatized so terribly. About a month later, one of the workers shared a story with me that was in the county newspaper and might have involved Itty Bitty Boo. Apparently, there was a man in the area who had adopted several cats from three different local animal shelters. One of the animal shelters had denied him from adopting a cat because he had just adopted a cat a month earlier from that same shelter. It turned out that he had adopted several cats from different shelters and was abusing all of them. The police found cats in his apartment with all kinds of injuries. Although there wasn't a picture of him in the newspaper article, I believed he was the same man I saw cutting the skin off of Itty Bitty Boo. He was later prosecuted on several counts of animal abuse based on the evidence in his apartment, though they could not directly link him to Itty Bitty Boo.

I had the pleasure of working with a beautiful four-year-old Great Dane. His coat was a soft gray-blue and as I looked into his crystal-blue eyes, I felt only gentleness. The shelter had named him Blue for his physical attributes, but the name suited his emotional state as well. The workers said he had been adopted but was returned about three weeks later for biting and being destructive. As I slipped my hands along his spine, he sat down and allowed me to give him energy. I saw him in the house by himself looking out the front window, and I heard him whining. Then I saw him pacing back and forth and tearing up a decorative pillow from a living room couch. It seemed like he had separation anxiety. Perhaps the owner mistook his anxious condition for bad behavior. I didn't see him bite anyone or anything other than a pillow.

I explained to the shelter worker that he needed to be with someone who didn't leave him alone for long periods of time. She noted it in his file and updated his card on his cage. Blue was eventually adopted by a man that owned a construction company and took him on all the jobs with him, so he wasn't left alone by himself.

As I gathered my belongings to leave one afternoon, the office manager asked me to scan a female Yorkshire terrier. The dog was scheduled to be spayed later in the week, and when they ran her preoperative bloodwork it showed an elevated white blood cell count, but they didn't know what was wrong with her. As I stood in front of the cage, the little Yorkie sat quietly and I put my hand up to her. All the energy was directed to her abdomen area. I felt in my own uterus intense pain, like there was some type of cyst there. She allowed me to work on her, even though she had pain and was trembling a bit. As soon as I disconnected from her energy, I no longer felt the pain. I told the shelter office manager what I felt, and then we went back to the veterinarian and I told her what happened with the dog. She said the dog was scheduled for her surgery the next day, so she would check it out. The following afternoon, the veterinarian called me at home. She said that when she went in to spay the little Yorkie, she found a pyometra. I didn't know what it was so she explained it as an infectious cyst of the uterus. She was able to remove it during the surgery. The dog was resting comfortably and was expected to make a good recovery.

While I was pregnant with my daughter, the shelter got in a group of seven puppies that were a mix between white German shepherd and golden retriever. Four of the puppies looked like golden retrievers and three looked like little baby polar bears. They were just a few weeks old, so they were in a restricted area not open to the public. I asked the shelter manager if I could adopt one. He said I could, but I had to wait until they were eight weeks old. Each week when I visited the shelter I spent time with my little white puppy. He was very gentle and in a cage with a much bigger male sibling than him who was eating all his food; the other dog was almost twice his size. While I worked on the other animals there, I would take my puppy out of the cage, feed him a little bit of food out of my hand, and let him run around in the room. He began to recognize my scent and whenever I went to the cage and put my hand up, he sniffed it and then licked my palm with his tiny pink tongue as his tail wagged happily from side to side like a metronome.

My OB/GYN advised me to stop visiting the shelter when I was seven months pregnant with Briella. He said I was at risk for Toxoplasmosis from working with cats. I had never heard of it because I never owned a cat, but apparently there is a parasite in cat feces that can cause a serious infection, which is why pregnant women are not supposed to clean their cats' litter pans. Although I assured my doctor that I wasn't cleaning cat litter pans, he said a cat could scratch me with the parasite in its nails from being in the litter pan. I felt sad about not being able to see all the animals regularly, but I didn't want to put myself at risk. The puppy that I wanted to adopt was eight weeks by that time, so I was able to take him home with me—a little piece of the shelter. Sampson became a new member of our family and Brayden loved his new buddy. I took a break from volunteering at the shelter until Briella was in preschool. It was bittersweet because I missed working with the animals, but I knew I would eventually get back to working with them.

After my first book came out, I had a client session with a woman named Roseanne Trezza. As soon as she walked through the door, I immediately recognized the blond-haired middle-aged woman. She had a youthful face and her beautiful blond hair framed it softly. I had met her once before at the Tinton Falls shelter. She was the executive director for the Associated Humane Society of New Jersey. I asked her if she remembered meeting me from the shelter. She said she didn't recall meeting me, but she was at a Barnes and Noble store and saw my book on display at the front counter. She said that she bought the book, read it in just a couple of days, and then looked up my website and saw that I had an office in New Jersey, so she booked an appointment.

I explained to her that I had been a volunteer at the Tinton Falls shelter for a couple of years, doing energy work with the animals there. She thought it was amazing that the universe had brought us together, and I honestly felt the same way. We had a great session. After the session I mentioned that if they needed help with the animals, I could help out with the Forked River shelter and Popcorn Park Zoo, both of which were just a few miles from my house. The Associated Humane Society ran three shelters in New Jersey. One was in Tinton Falls, one in Forked River, and one in Newark. In addition, the Associated Humane Society ran the Popcorn Park Zoo and wildlife rescue and sanctuary, a small 7-acre zoo with an attached clinic that provided homes to abandoned, injured, ill, exploited, abused, or elderly wildlife, exotic and farm animals, and birds. She said that would be great and she would talk to the Popcorn Park Zoo director, Dr. John Bergmann. A few days later she emailed me and said that John would love for me to visit the zoo and asked me to bring my children for a behind-the-scenes tour. We set up the meeting for two weeks out on an afternoon during the week.

As soon as we arrived, Roseanne met us outside and took all of us to the zoo gift shop. She had Popcorn Park Zoo sweatshirts for Brayden, Briella, and me. Then she took us inside the offices to meet John Bergmann, a medium-built man wearing khakis, a zoo sweatshirt, and a khaki sun hat. He was a kind man with a gentle smile and warm eyes. As soon as he greeted us, I immediately felt the compassion he exuded in his aura. This man was heart chakra–centered and put a great amount of love and compassion into everything he did.

He took us outside and through the gates to the back end of the zoo where pot-bellied pigs, peacocks, and geese welcomed us. Briella clung to my leg as a giant white goose came up next to her at eye level. John told the goose to step aside, and it did. We made our way to view the bobcats. A male bobcat walked over and sat down against the fence so John could pet him. John showed us the habitat of Dante the tiger. Then he called his name and the massive tiger rose from his den and sauntered to the edge of his run. He walked along the fence with us just a few steps behind John, keeping one eye on the rest of us the whole time. We walked across to the bigger lion/tiger area. John took us into the area where they feed the large cats. Caesar, an eleven-year-old male tiger, was rubbing his face against the fence and making loud noises like a playful cub. He seemed very excited to see John in the indoor area, and John spent some time rubbing Caesar's neck and talking to him. Brayden put his hand up to the fence to touch Caesar's face. I corrected him and explained that although Caesar was acting like a large domestic cat, he was a wild animal and we needed to respect his true nature. John had been his caretaker for years and had gained Caesar's trust. Brayden stepped back and nodded his head in agreement.

We went next door to the cougar domain to view one of the cougars. Camille, a female cougar, had had a seizure a couple of days earlier and was in a semi-zoned state. Although she was sitting up and conscious, she just stared at us without moving her head or any other body parts. It seemed like she wasn't "all there" and was perhaps a bit dizzy. John explained that after a seizure she was in that state for a couple of days, and then she would bounce back. Brayden put his hand up next to the cage and said he felt something in the front area of her head. I put my hand there and felt the same thing. It seemed like there was a bit of fluid there. John said they would have her examined. We gave her energy and tried to pull some of what was up in her head down to her feet.

The main animal that needed some energy balancing was Princess, the infamous twenty-seven-year-old camel who had been a zoo resident for over ten years. She was known for picking the winning NFL teams each week. John would write the name of competing teams on each hand and then put a graham cracker over each one. Whichever hand Princess ate from was her winning pick for that week. In 2013 she had successfully picked the winner of the Super Bowl. She chose the Baltimore Ravens, who defeated the San Francisco 49ers in a score of 34 to 31. There was a special place in my heart for this clairvoyant gentle giant, and I was excited to meet her up close.

When we entered her living area, she rose to her feet, standing over 10.5 feet tall from head to hoof, and greeted us by gracefully lowering her head. I felt a sense of reverence for her majestic presence. Brayden said that he was amazed at how large she was, yet she was so gentle. He immediately took to her and rubbed her muzzle. As I walked toward her, I suddenly felt achiness in all my bones but particularly in my hips and legs. I moved to the side of her and placed my hand on her hip. She glanced over at me and then knelt down and reclined on her knees. Brayden placed his hands on her other side.

"She has terrible pains in her legs," he said. He could feel all her ailments, just like me. Princess closed her eyes a bit and seemed relaxed by the energy. I mentioned to John that she had severe arthritis. He said they were aware of that and were giving her medication for it. I suggested that maybe they needed to increase it because I could feel her pain. I noted that eventually the pain would get to a point where she would not be able to get up and walk around anymore. John said that she had good days and bad days. I gave her more energy in her legs as she continued to munch on the graham crackers that Brayden fed her by hand.

Princess died about five months later. Her arthritis advanced and she couldn't stand up anymore, so she was euthanized. It was a very sad time for everyone at the zoo and all those who loved Princess. A huge part of the zoo's loving energy was gone. It was going to take some time for that huge void to be normalized. Brayden and I continue to visit the zoo quarterly. John usually has a list of animals he wants us to check in on. He's a closet clairsentient; he can feel things from the animals. Perhaps it is the amazing bond he has with all of them as their main caretaker. He has his views of what he thinks is happening with the animals, and often I confirm what he is already thinking about the relationships between the animals. It is amazing to observe the dynamic of the animals as this man walks through the zoo. All the animals walk to the edge of their habitats to greet him, including the massive 400-pound male tigers. These animals view him as the top of the hierarchy; he has won their trust. I admire John because he is a master at working with his staff and the animals—not many people can claim that skill set. It takes living from the heart-center daily to get to that advanced point in life. Brayden and I look forward to our continued work with the animals and all the lessons they teach us about growing in compassion.

EXERCISE

Clearing Your Energy Daily

We are always interacting with the energy of other people. Sometimes these interactions are good and sometimes they're not so good. These experiences can get imprinted in our aura and energetic field, as can the emotions we feel and project in response to the situations. It is a good idea to clear your energy regularly. I clear my energy and my children's energy each night before we go to bed. If you cannot do it daily, you should try to do it a couple of times a week. If you have a bad week where you experience a lot of negativity, you might want to clear multiple times.

We clear our energy so these negative experiences don't pull our vibrations down and keep us functioning at a low vibrational rate or frequency. Have you ever had a disagreement with a friend and then have difficulty sleeping that night because your mind is racing? You hear the argument over and over again in your head because it is imprinted in the mental layer of the aura. Or have you ever had someone close to you pass and for days after the funeral, you feel deeply saddened? This experience is imprinted in the emotional layer of the aura. Regardless of which auric layers are imprinted with these experiences, we want to clear them so they don't weigh down our energy and so we can function at our highest vibrational rate.

We can also pick up energy from places. People often complain of a toxic or negative work environment. Many people who work in a place that is not a vibrational fit for their energy may feel drained by the workplace or they may feel like they pick up negativity from it. If they choose to stay in a workplace that is not a vibrational fit, they will need to clear their energy regularly to release the imprints they are picking up so they do not bring that negativity home with them.

As you may know from my first book, *Discovering the Medium Within*, I'm a visual person, so I prefer visualization exercises because they are quick and easy. If you aren't a visual person, you can use physical methods of clearing your energy like smudging or using essences and essential oils. Whatever you choose, stick to it and get into a routine of clearing your energy regularly so you are always vibrating at your highest possible rate.

> *What you will need for this exercise:* your mind and a
> place to relax
>
> • • • •
>
> You can do this exercise standing straight up or
> lying down flat. I prefer to do it standing up.
>
> Using your third eye, visualize your aura. See it
> lit up and colorful.

Next, see a ray of violet light descending from above you.

As it descends, you feel the vibration of love permeating your aura. See the purple light coming down and enveloping you completely.

As the purple wave washes over you, it gently lifts everything other than the highest vibration of love from your entire energetic field.

Sense each imprint lifting and making you feel lighter.

When all imprints are removed from your field, we call in Saint Germain, the keeper of the violet flame, to transmute all energy into the highest vibration of love.

See the violet flame in its brilliance transmuting everything until there is only love.

Now see the violet light lifting from your aura and ascending above you.

Watch as it transforms into a colorful rainbow and then disappears into the sky.

Spend a moment and assess the differences in your energy. Do you feel lighter and more peaceful, balanced, and centered?

You may use this exercise whenever you need to clear imprints from your energy. It can be completed in under two minutes, and I recommend doing it daily.

• • • •

8

Spot Healing Treatments

I generally don't get sick. If I do, it's only for a couple of days and most of the time involves some type of energetic clearing that has a manifestation, such as a clearing of fear imprints that involves digestive upset. In our family we're always giving each other energy. Brayden is the only person that I allow to give me hands-on energy healing when I feel sick. Sometimes Briella helps out, but she loses interest in about ten minutes. I may ask my cousins to send me distance healing, and my guides in spirit work on me every night. It's always nice to feel their loving, warm energy. Brayden's energy is a strong, hot current and Briella's is more subtle and warm, generating out of her tiny hands.

We were at a baseball tournament in Pittsburgh, Pennsylvania, with Brayden and his travel team at the time. He was playing back-to-back games, but after the first game he had a bad headache.

"Ma, I need some energy. My head's killin' me." He sat on the bleachers and took off his hat. I put my hands on top of his head and sensed that an upper right vertebrae in his neck was out of alignment. I don't know if it was from pitching in the game or if it was from the way he slept. A few of his teammates came over to investigate the goings-on.

"What are you doin', Miss Anysia?" one of the boys asked.

"My mom's shifting my energy. She's a healing medium—she can help people heal, read energy, and talk to spirits," Brayden said matter-of-factly.

"No way," one of the other players said in a tone of disbelief.

"Yeah, she can. She wrote a book about it," Brayden said. He picked up my phone and showed the boys my phone case, which was a replica of the book's cover. The boys looked at it in amazement.

"She's the real deal, and I'm just like her," Brayden said. The boys asked me if it was true. I nodded my head in agreement and smiled. I listened quietly and kept shifting the energy in Brayden's neck. He said he felt a tingling sensation in that side of his neck and then the pain subsided. I continued to give him energy for a few more minutes, but then he needed to eat his lunch before the second game started.

"Is that better?" I asked. He rolled his neck to the right, to the left, and then back to the right again.

"It's good," he said.

Sometimes I experience neck pain after lifting weights, so I have Brayden give me energy to help align my spine. When I do incline chest flies, I often strain my neck to look up at the mirror to check my form. The next morning I would wake and my top couple of vertebrae would be out of alignment, plus the muscles in the area would be stiff. I would call to Brayden and he would put his hands on my shoulder or side of my neck and I would immediately feel the energy pulsating out of his hands and into my neck. It felt like a massage of warm energy. Soon the muscles would loosen, my neck would shift back to normal, and Brayden could feel that his job was done for the time being.

My friend visited from San Francisco with her family and we were going to her mom's house in Island Heights for dinner. Mrs. Gajano has a large five-bedroom Craftsman Victorian home that was built in 1917. We always enjoy going there because she spent twenty years living in Italy and is an amazing cook. She specializes in preparing Italian food but has traveled the world and can cook all types of intercontinental specialties. That night she had prepared lasagna with a beautiful fresh salad. Before dinner we sat outside on the screened-in porch that ran along the front of the house. It was wonderful to see everyone; we shared stories and caught up on our lives.

Everyone took their seats around the long rectangular table, which was beautifully dressed in linens and bone china. As I scanned the dimly lit room, I saw smiling faces and felt so much love. That's the thing about Mrs. Gajano's house: it is filled with love, and love is imprinted in the walls and floorboards. When she was a child it was the summer residence of her parents, and when she returned from Italy, she lived in the grand home year-round. Since that time it had become the family's central gathering point. On any given night three or four cousins or friends would just stop in to visit. The door was always open to family and friends. The dining room was a special place where people would sit and enjoy each other's company for hours over long meals and spirited conversation.

There was something special about Mrs. Gajano's house from being the family grounding post for almost a century. Everyone was attached to its comfort and nostalgia, but no one loved it more than Mrs. Gajano, who, at eighty-three years old, insisted that her home in Island Heights was still her favorite place out of all the places in the world she had traveled to.

We enjoyed the delicious meal of salad with strawberries and avocado and the main course of homemade lasagna. Dinnertime was more than a quick meal in her house. It was time for everyone to enjoy each other—to slow down from their busy lives and spend a few hours nurturing the body and soul with good food, lots of love, and a bit of laughter. It was really a lost art form, at least in the United States, where fast food ruled our lives and families were always busy running children to activities and didn't often have time for a family meal around the table together.

After dinner we cleared the dishes and set the table for dessert. I brought red velvet cupcakes—a favorite sweet of both my children. Mrs. Gajano had prepared a ripe summer fruit salad. She scooped vanilla ice cream for the children and drizzled the fresh fruit over the frosty mounds. She had an ice cream cake and a crystal bowl of mixed nuts also on the table. After everyone sat down, Mrs. Gajano came into the room with her infamous crema di limoncello and manderino liqueurs—both homemade from freshly picked lemons and mandarin oranges grown in California. I loved the manderino because it wasn't an overpowering orange flavor; it tasted like a sweetened tangerine. We enjoyed our dessert, talking and laughing for another hour or so.

When we cleared the table from dessert, Mrs. Gajano asked me to look at her left calf because she was experiencing some swelling and was wearing a compression stocking on the leg. She sat down on the kitchen chair and I stood behind her and placed both of my hands on her shoulders. I could feel the heavy pressure in the leg and it seemed sore, like the tissues were being stretched to hold all the excess fluid accumulating there. The fluid quickly began draining down toward the left ankle, but I wanted to know why the fluid was accumulating there. As I moved my hand upward on her back, it settled over her left kidney. I could feel the energy was moving slowly there, and when I silently asked what it was about, I heard that she was dealing with some fears about her own mortality and making sure everyone in her family was okay. She worried about her children, though they were all grown adults. She wished that her daughter in Italy would move to the United States so she could be in close proximity to her other siblings. As I worked on the fears stored in the kidneys, I could feel some pain in my low back. Mrs. Gajano commented that her back was hurting her a bit that day. She said she could feel the heated energy in her back and it felt like it was massaging all the muscles.

Just then Brayden came in the kitchen and asked for another piece of ice cream cake. We had already put the cake in the freezer, but it wasn't a problem to take it out and slice him another piece. I told him he could have another one but he needed to give Mrs. Gajano some energy first. He sat on the wooden chair across from her and placed his hands on her knees.

He said, "Wow, my back hurts. You have a definite issue in your low back. It's sore on the left side. You need to get that looked at." She commented on how hot Brayden's hands felt on her knees. I told Brayden that she did have an issue in her low back, and Mrs. Gajano agreed. I told him that he needed to ground her energy and pull it down to her feet. Whenever we worked on anyone, their energy would shift higher and then we could move things around. When we were done with the healing, we needed to ground their energy and pull it back down to the earth so they wouldn't be dizzy or feel flighty and disconnected from their bodies. He spent a minute pulling the energy down to her ankles.

"There, I grounded her through her feet. Can I have a piece of cake now?" he asked with a straight face. Everyone in the kitchen burst out laughing because he was so matter-of-fact about it. Healing was such a normal part of his life, just like eating. Although we found great humor in how Brayden jumped from healing right back into eating cake, I found that moment quite telling. I realized that I was raising him to use his abilities in daily life and see them as normal. When he was very little and I knew he had the same abilities as me, I made a commitment to teach him that it was okay to be this way. Brayden is the reason why I embraced my abilities; I didn't want him to grow up like me, where I was always told by my family to never tell anyone I could see or communicate with spirits. I was basically taught that it was wrong to be myself. I never wanted Brayden to feel that way. At that moment in Mrs. Gajano's kitchen, I felt joy because I had taught him well and he was grounded and good with being himself. I just validated for me that he was a very special soul.

Before we left that night, Mrs. Gajano hugged us and said she felt so relaxed and the pain had subsided in her leg; she couldn't wait to go to bed and get a good night's sleep without the leg pain. We thanked her for a wonderful evening, and I told her that she would probably be very tired later because there was a lot of stuff shifting in her energy.

The next day, Mrs. Gajano called me and said the swelling in her leg was completely gone, her back felt great, and she wasn't wearing the compression stocking. She thanked me and told me to thank Brayden for healing her. I reminded her that we were just facilitators. She is the one that allowed the divine energy in; in fact, she had healed herself. After I got off the phone, I said a prayer thanking God for not only being able to be part of the healing process of others but also for my son. I was so very grateful that God had sent Brayden to me to help me remember who I really was on a soul level and to remind me of why I came to the earth.

EXERCISE

Grounding Our Hands

We need to ground our energy regularly. There are a variety of methods we can use to ground ourselves. Most entail the energy flowing downward from the crown chakra through the other major chakras and into the earth. By connecting ourselves to the earth, we can ensure that we are fully present in the moment.

We all use our hands daily, and we all have hand chakras in the center of our palms. Our hands constantly interact with the energy of others through physical contact. Whether we shake hands, hug others, or hold the door for someone, our hands are always conducting and sensing energy all day long. If we want to stay connected with the earth, why not specifically ground the part of the body conducting the most energy?

Grounding hands gives us an immediate and solid connection to the earth. It only takes a couple of minutes and can be used in conjunction with the body grounding exercise on page 88 or as a standalone method. All energy workers especially should ground their hands daily, but really we should all ground our hands regularly because we are constantly exchanging energy with others and picking up energetic imprints through our hands.

If you favor physical methods, you can ground your hands by briefly holding a grounding stone in each hand. There are several grounding stones that have a strong magnetic current such as black obsidian, hematite, and onyx. Holding a small piece of one of these stones will immediately ground the hand chakra in the center of the palm, and it will also pull the energy downward and ground the body. You can also walk outside and connect your hands directly to grass, dirt, or sand, and your hand chakras will be immediately grounded. You can also use a visualization method to quickly ground your hands. One of my favorite visualization methods is a quick exercise involving visualizing cords from the hands.

What you will need for this exercise: your mind

• • • •

Close your eyes and visualize your hand chakras in the center of your palms. See and feel them spinning and energized.

Envision a long brown cord coming from the left palm and extending down to the ground.

As the cord connects to the earth, see it take root and grow. See green leaves growing from it, and feel all the energy in your palm pulled down and connected to the earth.

Envision a long brown cord coming from the right palm and extending down to the ground.

As the cord connects to the earth, see it take root and grow. See green leaves growing from it, and feel all the energy in your palm pulled down and connected to the earth.

Now that both palms are connected to the earth, pull some energy up the cords and allow the hand chakras to be filled with this energy from the earth. Feel it balancing both hand chakras.

When you feel the hand chakras are balanced, you can visually see both cords disconnecting from your palms and falling to the ground. Watch as the cords are absorbed into the dirt, and see how the leaves on them grow into two strands of deep green ivy that will continue to grow and are strongly rooted in the earth.

• • • •

9

Clearing Addictions

Sometimes we meet people and the connection intrinsically clicks into place like a key to a lock opening the door to something amazing. Melissa had been my brother Kyle's friend for several years. A hairstylist by trade, the petite Italian beauty with her long brown flowing hair had big brown eyes to match. She had many male friends because she was an expert in cutting the Brooklyn Fade, a style that's tight and tapered from the sides and back and then spiked at the top. They all needed her styling expertise so they could be in with the trend, but she was a best friend to my brother. I figured if she could keep Kyle in check, I had to meet her. He spoke often of her, but it wasn't until my hairdresser moved out of state that we actually met in person.

I walked into the hair salon in the mall lined with young female stylists, all of whom were in their early twenties and dressed in black like they had just left a wake for a family member. The receptionist led me to the last station on the right side. The bubbly little brunette stepped out from behind a wall and greeted me.

.'m Melissa," she said, swiveling the styling chair around so
_ould sit in it. "I've know Kyle forever, and he talks about you
all the time, so I feel like I know you already," she said, giggling.
I laughed too because I felt the same way. Kyle always told me
Melissa stories. Ironically, our hair was similar in style, color,
and texture, so she was the perfect person to know exactly what
I needed.

"What's with the black clothes on everyone?" I asked.

"Oh, we don't have uniforms, but they want us wearing a
black top and bottom so it looks professional," she said with a
smirk.

"I guess it's professional if you're a mortician or work in a
funeral parlor," I said.

"I know, right? It's a little depressing. It'd be better if we
wore a bright color, but everyone looks good in black," she commented.

As she trimmed my hair we joked about my little brother and
talked about my family. She knew all my siblings and parents
through Kyle. I loved her energy. She was upbeat, funny, and
a little sarcastic. She seemed like she could be related to me in
some way because I felt like I had known her forever. We chatted
together like we were the only people in the busy salon as she
blew out and styled my hair beautifully. She had a knack for styling and had definitely found her calling.

After that encounter, Melissa became my stylist and the seeds
of friendship sprouted. I would visit her every couple of months
and we would catch up on our lives. Each time I visited her,
it was as if I had seen her yesterday. I saw in Melissa a light
that could shine through anything. She was fearless, honest, and

spunky; plus, she was totally real and not afraid to be herself. It was all out there and I could totally be myself with her always. She was an unconditional person—a rare find, like deep blue sea glass along the shoreline.

Melissa's connection to my brother really became evident when he was diagnosed with cancer. Everyone struggled when Kyle got sick. He was charismatic and had a lasting effect on people, but for those closest to him, the pain cut a bit deeper. One night my phone rang at 11:30 and it was Melissa. As soon as I answered the phone, I could feel sadness and a bit of anxiety in her energy.

At first, we talked about our fears with Kyle's illness.

"I feel like I should do something for your brother, but I don't know what I can do. I feel helpless," she said. I knew what she meant because I felt the same way. I listened to her concerns. Then I explained that it was Kyle's battle and we had to let him work through it. We could control our emotions and provide emotional support and love to him, but that was all we could do. The tone lightened and we discussed Kyle's upcoming cancer benefit at the Bamboo Bar.

"Maybe we could have an auction at the benefit. I know so many salon owners; I could get them to donate baskets of supplies and gift certificates," she said. It was a great idea. Melissa's dad owned a salon in Holmdel, and she was well connected in that industry. She also said that she could get the other girls in her salon to help solicit donations. All the girls there knew my brother and loved him.

Including a gift auction was a fantastic idea, and I agreed to write the donation solicitation letter. We made a list of all the places to solicit. I took notes during the conversation so we had a follow-up reference point. The next day I typed up the letter and dropped off copies at the salon for the hairdressers. Melissa said she would collect all the donations and store them in her condo, and then we would wrap them at my house a couple of days before the event. In the meantime, I took Kyle to see my accountant to go over the potential event funds. I wanted to make sure we were doing everything correctly according to IRS standards. She advised us on how to handle all the financial gifts from the event.

My family members collected and donated a bunch of auction items, and the salon hairdressers went to local businesses and solicited donations. The night before the event, Melissa came over along with my mom, sister, and Kyle. We coordinated all the baskets and wrapped them in cellophane with bows. My den looked like a city street after a ticker tape parade, with colored paper fill, tape, cellophane, and price tags strewn across the den run and wooden floor. When we were done around 2:00 a.m., we had over 125 gift baskets for the event ready and wrapped. Each gift basket had a testicular cancer screen card from the Sean Kimerling Testicular Foundation and a cancer support card from the American Cancer Society. I knew the audience would have a lot of young men my brother's age. If we could help one person detect testicular cancer early, we were making a difference.

People went nuts over the gift baskets at the auction. You could hear a pin drop when the bar manager pulled winning numbers from the buckets. The entire event raised a lot of money for Kyle's medicine and medical care. At the end of the night, Melissa and I sat down and rested because we had had two insanely busy days that were running into each other, only separated by a few hours of sleep. It was just another sprinkling of love and joy that fed our friendship as it blossomed.

Shortly after Kyle's event, though, I noticed a subtle change in Melissa. She seemed a little sad and distant, and her smile faded. When I went to get my hair done, I asked her what was bothering her. She said she was working two jobs and was really tired. She worked at the salon in the mall, but she was also managing her dad's salon a few days a week and it was an hour away from her home. Plus she dated a guy who I felt drained her a bit. Although he seemed nice, he didn't work much. A few weeks later, I knew something was up because I contacted Melissa to try to get together for lunch and she never responded. I wanted to talk to her in detail about what I was picking up in her energy. I figured she needed some space, so I gave it some time. I made another appointment to get my hair done with the salon rather than through texting Melissa. When I got to the salon, Melissa looked drained. The dark circles under her eyes matched her black shirt and pants, giving her an overall pallid appearance. She tried to be bubbly with me, but I could see through to her sadness.

"How are you?" I asked abruptly.

"I'm great," she said.

Total bullshit, I thought to myself as I smiled politely at her and nodded my head. The conversation between us flowed slowly; like old crystallized honey oozing out of a jar, it was awkward and stagnant. A couple of times Melissa completely spaced out and lost track of what she was saying. When I left I told her I would see her soon.

As I stepped into the parking lot, I called my brother and asked him what was wrong with Melissa; she was totally out of it and not herself. He said the guy she was dating was a drug addict, and he thought that Melissa had got herself involved in taking prescription pills. It was more than a little problem. Her personality was completely altered, and I felt like she was lost.

A couple of weeks later, I contacted Melissa to get a blowout for my hair because I was going to New York for an interview but I had to be in the city early in the morning. Melissa said I could come to her condo the night before the event.

When I got to the condo, her boyfriend greeted me in his sweatpants and tattered T-shirt. He said Melissa wasn't home from work yet but I could hang out in the den until she got there. I sat across from him and scanned his energy as he ate a burrito and refried beans from a Styrofoam takeout container while watching an episode of MTV's *Cribs*.

"No work today?" I asked flatly.

"Nah, I only help out with my family's restaurant when they need me, so I'm off a lot," he replied.

What a lazy slug. Man up! I thought. Meanwhile, Melissa was working at two different hair salons, one of which had an hour commute each way, and she had taken on a third job bartending a few nights a week at a bar on the boardwalk, and this guy was lying around her condo all day doing basically nothing. His energy repulsed me and I actually felt my stomach turning in disgust as I sat across the room from him. Melissa came home about fifteen minutes after I arrived.

"Sorry, I had a late client," she said.

"It's okay," I replied as she led me back to the second bedroom, which she had converted into a mini salon. Her expressionless face and rundown appearance conveyed the spirit of a depressed person who was barely functioning and surviving in autopilot mode. Her energy looked much darker and felt heavier than it was the last time I had seen her. She sprayed my hair down to wet it, then began styling it. She didn't say much. I kept the conversation light, with simple questions that required only yes or no responses. I paid Melissa and thanked her. She wished me luck in my interview. We hugged and then I headed out her door. The visit was very different from our usual encounters, but I knew she was tired from her long day. I told myself that I would check in on her the following day, after she had a good night's sleep.

On the way home, when I drove on the parkway, a car came speeding behind me with the lights flashing. I was in the middle lane and the car could have passed on the left, but it continued to tailgate so I moved my car to the far right lane. As I did this, the car came up alongside me and sideswiped the left front of my navy blue BMW—as it hit my car, I recorded the license plate in my mind. I got off at the next exit and wrote down the plate number, then I dialed 911. The local police arrived right away, as did a New Jersey state trooper, since the accident had occurred on a state highway. The trooper took the report and made note of the dark gray paint transfer on my blue car. The license plate came up valid and registered to an address in a town a few miles away. The trooper was going to the address and said I could pick up the report the following day. Eventually it was resolved because the trooper found evidence at the driver's home of paint transfer from my car to the other car and the damage was in line with what I had reported. My insurance covered my damages, and the other driver received tickets for careless driving, leaving the scene of an accident, and failure to report an accident.

When I got to my house, I messaged Melissa and told her what had happened to me on the way home from her condo. She couldn't believe it and asked if I got hurt. I assured her that I was fine but there was a bit of a dent in the side of my car and paint from the other car. We joked about what a crazy night it had been for both of us.

Then Melissa asked me for advice. She said that she had been feeling depressed and didn't know what to do about it. I told her that I had noticed it in her and was glad that she had opened up and trusted me with such a vulnerable situation. It was a sign of the strength of our friendship. To this day, Melissa still has that message saved. I wrote back to her with these exact words:

> It is a decision you have to make but I can tell you that the self-medicating is only masking the depression issue. At the root of the issue is the fact that you are very unhappy with where you are in life. You thought you would be married with a child and owning your own home right now. You do not see any way out of the situation and the pills make it all a blur and you can go through the motions, but when they wear off, it is right there in front of you again and there is also some physical back pain as well. But the real issue is emotional. You are a good person with a good heart. You have to get out of this rut. You might want to have a discussion with your father. He might be more receptive about it than your mom. You have been in a dark place and you need to step into the light. I am sending you

light and love and hope that you make the best decision
for yourself.

Melissa thanked me and said she would give it a lot of thought
before making a decision on how to move forward. Although
we had never actually talked about her prescription pill problem prior to that message exchange, she knew I could pick up
on everything in her energy: good, bad, or indifferent. If it was
there, I could perceive it. I sent her some energy that night for
whatever was in her highest intentions. I also sent her some loving energy because I felt her vibration was so low that she could
not perceive love easily, and I wanted her to know that no matter
how great the darkness, there was always love around her.

A few months later Melissa and I got word that a mutual
friend had died suddenly. I contacted Melissa and invited her
to drive to the funeral viewing with me. I agreed to pick her up
at the salon at 7:30 p.m. Melissa wasn't outside when I arrived.
She kept texting me saying she was on her way. I waited forty-five minutes in the mall parking lot. I felt annoyed because
the viewing was only until 9:00 p.m. and we still had a twen-
ty-minute drive. When she finally came out, she apologized and
put all of her things in the back seat. I could feel that her issue
wasn't resolved. We kept the conversation short on the drive
up, joking about my brother and the goofy things he always
says. We arrived in just under twenty minutes, with less than a
half hour before the viewing's end. It was a very sad event. The
viewing of a young person is always difficult because we expect
everyone to live until they're old and gray, plus a sudden passing
robs people of closure. We both walked up to the casket and said
a prayer together, and then we shared our condolences with the

family members. As we left I felt that it was a good time to talk to Melissa about her drug addiction.

We pulled out of the parking lot and sat for a minute at a red traffic light.

"I'm very worried about you," I said. She looked forward and lowered her head a bit.

"Don't judge me," Melissa said defensively. I said that I would never judge anyone with an addiction issue because I don't know what her life experiences had been. I also noted that several of the younger members in my family had struggled with addiction issues in the past, and I had deep compassion for anyone battling through darkness. Melissa listened quietly. I didn't lecture. I spoke to her like a sister. I told her I loved her and was worried about her well-being.

She said that her boyfriend's mother thought they should get married. She asked what I thought about it.

"You wanna know what your life will be like if you marry this guy? It'll be just like what it is now. You'll be working your butt off and he'll be sitting home leeching off you and draining every ounce of your energy." She frowned and looked out the window. "I'm not saying that to be mean. I'm saying it because I love you and want to see you happy in life. He's not good for you; he's a taker. You have to get away from him and the drugs. You need to talk to your dad."

"I can't talk to my dad. I'm not close enough to share this with him. I don't need him telling me how disappointed he is in me," Melissa said. Melissa's parents were divorced, and her father was engaged. Melissa was naturally closer to her mother.

"I'm sure he'd rather be disappointed in you than see something terrible happen to you from drugs. He loves you. He would do anything to help you." I saw a tear glisten down her cheek, and she quickly brushed it away with her fingers. "Please talk to your dad," I pleaded.

"Fine. I'll find a time and talk to him," she said. I made her promise me, and she agreed. I told her that if she didn't talk to him, I would come to her condo and kick her butt like a football across town. She laughed as I pulled into her condo parking lot.

I told her, "I love ya, and I wanna see you live your dream of being married to a wonderful man and being a mom to your children."

"Me too," she said. Then we hugged and she got out of the car and walked to her condo. When she reached the door, I pulled away and beeped the car horn.

Melissa drove to Florida with her father and his fiancée for Christmas that year. During the trip her father commented several times that she seemed different and not like herself. Melissa played it off. But a couple of weeks later, in January, he made her go to dinner with him. At the dinner Melissa came clean with her father and told him about her prescription drug problem. He immediately enrolled her in a drug rehab in Florida. I didn't speak to her before she left, but Melissa told my brother that I made her tell her dad the truth. I confirmed that I had, in fact, tried to get her to have the conversation with her dad, but ultimately it was Melissa who had decided she needed help.

Though I didn't hear from her for a few months, I sent energy to Melissa each week for whatever was in her highest intentions. As the weeks passed, I could feel her energy becoming lighter and more vibrant than before. I knew she was getting better and choosing to move forward in her life. I got word that she was working in a salon along the riverfront. I texted Melissa to see if I could visit her and get my hair done. She was excited to hear from me and told me to come in a couple of days later. When I walked into the reception area, Melissa—the one that I had always known, with her bubbly personality and beautiful light in her soul—greeted me with a big smile. We hugged, and we both had tears in our eyes. Her station was in the back of the salon. She shared it with another hairdresser, but the woman was at lunch during my appointment. It worked out well because it afforded us an opportunity to speak candidly.

"How are you?" I asked.

"I'm doing better. Thanks for helping me because you were the one who told me to go to my dad, and I did," she said.

"I'm just glad you're healthy and okay," I said.

"I feel better, but I think I need a healing session because I still feel like there's darkness biting at my heels. It seems like it's always there waiting for me to go back to the addiction; it's so dark, like a sense of evil." Melissa was now living by her dad. He did not want her to return to Toms River because that is where her drug use began. Of course, once she went into rehab, she cut ties with her slug boyfriend, but she still needed to rid herself completely of the drug energy.

I knew what Melissa was talking about because addiction involved dark energetic attachments that were always lurking and working on the subconscious mind of the person trying to get them to use. I had seen it with other clients who had drug addictions. Depending on the level of the addiction, the person may also have attracted energetic attachments to the aura.

Often, if we do not help cross those who have passed of substance overdose deaths, they can remain earthbound and walk in darkness, similar to suicide victims. These earthbound energies can attach and manipulate human substance abusers. These entities will still seek out addiction energy because, though they have passed on, they are still attached to the earth. They will attach themselves to the field of a user so they can still connect to the energy of the substance involved in the addiction. The entities can affect the user by sending thoughts of using, so that the user is always in an addictive state and the entity is always feeling the energy of the high. The person using the drugs or other substances always had a weakness in their personality, whether it was depression, self-medicating, lack of self-love, or low self-esteem. This weakness is what allowed the energy to attach. At first it is subtle, and then it grows in its ability to influence the person, until they became numb and disconnected from life.

While Melissa cut my hair, I suggested that she come to my office a few days later for a session. She said that she felt it was necessary to complete the healing work she began at rehab.

"I just want to clear any bit of the darkness that is still around me. I want it all gone," she said.

"I know what you mean. If it's your intention to clear it in the session, it will go because energy follows intention," I said.

A few nights later Melissa came to my office for her session. As we ascended the stairs she admitted that she was a little nervous. At the time we had known each other for nine years. I couldn't imagine what she would be afraid of with me.

"I'm not nervous about you. I'm nervous about the process. It's my first session; I don't know what to expect," she said.

"Don't be! Everything will happen as it should, and it's all for your highest good," I added. She smiled as I unlocked the door to my office. As we stepped through the doorway, her eyes widened.

"I love this place. It's so peaceful," she commented.

"Thanks. That's the energy I was trying to achieve here." She walked around and looked at all the angels in various sizes and colors on the cabinetry. Some were holding objects such as hearts or doves, and some had words on them like *believe, love,* and *faith.*

"I love all the plants and greenery. It makes the room feel alive and energized in a good way," she commented. I was glad she felt the natural vibe of the plants. I thought they gave the space a very comfortable feeling as well. As we sat at the wicker table, I explained what she could expect in the healing session. She listened intently. A couple of times her eyes got big and she laughed a bit, but, for the most part, Melissa knew a great deal about my work.

We made our way to the massage table. Melissa had to use the little white wooden footstool because the table was too high for her, as she was a little shorty. She pulled the covers up to her neck and joked about falling asleep in the session. I assured her that she wouldn't fall asleep. As soon as I said the opening prayer, I could feel the heaviness Melissa had mentioned. It was thick and dark and imprinted in the layers of her aura.

We cleared it and she immediately felt lighter. I explained to Melissa that addiction could sometimes also have dark energetic or low-vibration attachments. The dark, heavy energy I cleared from her aura was imprinted from the drug addiction. Basically, with those imprints in the aura, it was like a calling card for low-vibrational energy to attach and influence her thoughts. Melissa said that was exactly how she felt—as if someone was taunting her to use drugs again.

At the time of the session there were no attachments to her aura. If she had them, I would have made her aware of them and asked her to consciously choose to release them and raise her vibration, so they could no longer attach to her field. Attachments can only stick to your aura if part of your energetic field is vibrating at a rate low enough for them to attach. So, in a way, attachments can actually call your attention to what needs to be healed in your energy. But if you are unaware that they are there, they can have a strong influence over you.

"I feel like they are just there waiting for me to fail again," she said.

"You won't fail again. You have worked too hard to get into this light; you won't go back to the darkness," I said. Melissa nodded her head in agreement. I knew that Melissa had to choose to stay in the light. But I also knew that if she didn't clear the imprints in her aura, she could regress and pick up attachments. I had experienced this with other drug-addicted clients and most closely with a cousin of mine who battles a heroin addiction. I chose to send her energy one day because a family member had told me that she was not doing well. That night after I cleared the energy of myself, everyone in my home, and my home, I decided to clear her energy and send her light—*big mistake!* As I connected with her energy, it felt very heavy and looked dark. A few minutes later I had a large dark entity in my room. Although it could not attach to me because it vibrated at a very low rate and was not a vibrational fit for my energy, it hovered around me. I tried clearing it and it didn't budge, so I called in my spirit guides and asked what it was about.

I was told that we cannot clear what a person has chosen for themselves. My cousin had chosen to be in that dark state. She might not have chosen that darkness at first, but as the addiction grew she chose to keep using, so her energy vibrated lower and lower, and the dark entity became attached. I could not force her to clear that darkness and step into the light; she had to want to do that for herself. Rather than just sending her loving energy for whatever was in her highest intentions, I chose to send her light to clear her field; I had sent her energy with my own intentions for her, which was an energetic faux pas. I did not have the right to clear her. That was up to her, and I had basically imposed my will upon her. I chose to connect with her energy, so I got everything that came with that energy, including her dark attachment. My guides helped me clear the dark attachment, and I learned a very big lesson about energetic attachments and addiction. Melissa had already cleared her attachments before her session by choosing to stop using drugs and raising her vibration, but we still needed to clear the dark imprints in her energetic field.

There was a lot of balancing and clearing in the session. One area where we spent some time was the sacral chakra. Melissa was afraid that she would never be able to have children because of the toxins she had put in her body.

"I just feel like I won't ever be able to have children when I finally meet someone I love," she said. As I worked in her sacral chakra, I balanced it. I didn't see any blockages, and I told her to let go of that thoughtform because it was fear based. She agreed to let it go. I moved up to the solar plexus, where her personal power and self-esteem were stored. I heard an imprint there attached to both the mental and emotional bodies. I heard, "I'm a failure." I called this to her attention. She said that it was something she struggled with because she felt she had failed herself by using drugs. I told her it had to go because that is the type of imprint that could attract low-vibrational attachments.

"Get rid of it. I definitely don't want it there," she said. We pulled it out, and she said she felt the area get very cold and she had chills afterwards. I explained that people sometimes feel that sensation after releasing something from the energetic field. She nuzzled herself under the blanket and pulled the edge up to her chin. Then an elderly couple in spirit visited at the corner of the room. They identified themselves as her paternal great grandparents. I asked Melissa for permission to allow them in the session. She agreed.

They told her they were proud of how she had overcome the struggle with addiction. Her great grandmother said it was a sign of how much strength she held within her little body. Her great grandparents said they would watch over and guide her as she continued on her journey. They went on to talk a little bit about her father, including things spanning from when he was a little boy to his adulthood. Melissa validated all the things they shared. They stayed for the duration of the session, but I kept focused on where I needed to go in her energy. I moved up to the heart chakra, in the center of the chest. As soon as I placed my hand there I felt deep sadness, including despair. It seemed like she felt unloved. I told her what I felt there and asked her if it was true.

She cried. "I feel like who would love me after what I've been through? I don't even love myself."

"I love you," I said tearfully as I reached out and hugged her.

I knew I needed to connect her to her higher self. It was an exercise that I only used in sessions where people had been suicidal, were working through serious addiction issues, or felt really unloved and lost in this life. I explained to Melissa that we were going to do a brief meditation, and all she needed to do was close her eyes and relax while following my lead. I told her that the higher self was the perfect version of ourselves that resided in the divine realm. It was the part of our soul that was in spirit form and watched over the human self and guided us on our soul path. Sometimes we blocked the connection with the higher self and could feel deep sadness, loneliness, or unloved. But once we cleared the blockage, we would feel the unconditional love that flowed like a gentle river from the divine realm. Melissa said that she was excited to do the exercise.

As she closed her eyes I had her breathe deeply and slowly. We did this for a few breaths. Then she began relaxing all the muscles in her body one at a time, from the head down to the feet. Next, I had her envision a golden cord running from the center of her chest, in the heart chakra, and going up through the center of her body, through the top of her head, and out the crown chakra. As the cord ascended to the heavens, she was sending love from the heart chakra. The cord eventually reached the divine realm and connected to the higher self. Once attached, the higher self sent love down the cord back to Melissa. I told her to allow the love to fill her heart chakra completely and then let it spill out and fill all the areas in her body that needed love. As she did this I saw tears slip out from under her eyelids and glisten in the dim light of the salt lamps.

Little by little, the cord shortened and the higher self drew closer to the human self. At last the higher self was present, and then I guided Melissa to communicate telepathically with her higher self. I told her to ask the higher self what guidance she had to share, and I instructed her to spend a few minutes communicating with her higher self. Melissa cried while she communicated with her higher self, and she let the tears flow down her cheeks. After a couple of minutes we sent the higher self back to the divine realm via the golden cord. I explained that the higher self would remain in the divine realm until the human self was vibrating at the same rate as that of the higher self. The human self has to transcend the ego and live fully in the vibration of unconditional love. Once it reaches this point, the human self and higher self merge and are an embodiment of pure divine love. I reminded Melissa that she could always do this exercise whenever she needed to feel loved or supported in this life.

"That was totally amazing. I never felt so much love in my life," she commented.

"The connection to the love is always there for us; we just need to tune in to it," I said. Melissa said that she felt amazing and that the higher self not only told her to love, but also to forgive herself because the addiction was a necessary part of her journey. She seemed overwhelmed by the connection of love from the higher self. She kept her eyes closed as I continued to balance her energy and finished the session with a smile on her face. When she got off the table and stood on the footstool, I guided her to the floor. I explained that this work would make her feel a little dizzy.

"I feel it—like I'm spinning a bit," she commented.

"When we do this work, we shift your energy to a high frequency, kind of like the vibration of a spirit, so we can move things around and clear them. When we are done, your frequency slows down back to an earthly vibration. As it slows down, you feel a little off balance. I'm going to put my hands on your shoulders and pull all your energy down from your head to your feet. We call this grounding, and it is going to feel like you get very heavy," I explained. Melissa nodded her head in agreement, and then I placed my hands on her shoulders and grounded her.

"Wow. I feel like I weigh five hundred pounds," she said after I grounded her. She took a seat on the bench across from the table. She sat silently for a few seconds as I pulled the sheets off the table.

"I feel amazing—so much lighter. I can't believe it," she said as she laced her sneakers. I explained about the post-healing balancing and clearing she would experience over the next week. She listened and took it all in. I could see the change in her energy already. She was much lighter and happier. She had let it all go.

A month after her healing, Melissa reconnected with a friend from high school named Frank. They had dated when they were twenty-one, but it had been a busy time for both of them and it hadn't worked out. Once they reconnected, he invited her out to dinner and they started dating again. He was really nice to her and she enjoyed spending time with him. I knew he was the man she would marry, but I didn't tell her; it was too early to share that information. A few months later I visited Melissa, and she told me she was pregnant. She was happy about it but a little bit nervous, too. I was very excited for her and kept calling her "little mommy."

"I blame you 'cause you cleared all my crap out and then I got pregnant right away," she said.

"Do ya? 'Cause I'm pretty sure I wasn't around when *that* happened," I said as I pointed to her stomach. She laughed, and so did I. "You should be thrilled. Do you remember from your session? That was your biggest fear."

She smiled and said, "I'm happy. I was so afraid I would never get pregnant, and look at me now. We're gonna get married, but everything's happening so fast." We talked a little bit about what she had going on, and we diffused some of her fears. She was finally moving toward the life she had always wanted. Of course, the timing wasn't exactly as she had imagined, but then again, nothing ever happens in our time; it's always in divine time.

On October 2 of that year, Melissa and Frank delivered Lilliana, a tiny jet-black-haired princess. She texted me pictures of the baby swaddled in pink blankets from the hospital, and I could feel the joy she had for her new baby girl. At the time we were driving home from the American Girl store in New

York City. I had just held a party in the restaurant there celebrating Briella's fifth birthday with my family. I thought Briella and I would be going back there someday with Melissa and Lilliana. Briella was so excited to see the pictures of the baby and couldn't wait until she was old enough to babysit her.

About a year after Lilliana's birth, Melissa and Frank celebrated their wedding at a place called Nanina's in the Park. It's a big place for Italian weddings, and they do it right! At the time my diet was limited because I was training for a fitness competition to be held two weeks after the wedding, but my brother enjoyed all the delicacies.

I honestly had never seen Melissa look more beautiful. Her hair was down in long curled tendrils, and her radiance was amplified against her white dress. It wasn't until dinnertime that I got to greet her. She had made her rounds to some of the tables with Frank, but I had missed her because I was in the bathroom. When she finally took her seat at the head table, I went over to see her. She stood up and hugged me. I told her that I was so proud of her. She was a true Cinderella story, except instead of being rescued by a prince, she had rescued herself.

"I can't believe it either," she said.

"You did it, and I am so proud of you. I admire your courage," I said as I watched the biggest smile grow across her face. She reached out and hugged me.

We don't always get to witness or be part of such amazing transformations in life, but when we're gifted with a brief glimpse, we realize they're truly miraculous and with the help of divine light, all things are possible. Melissa was in the darkest place and barely alive, living day in and day out like an emotionless robot, but she chose to clear her darkness and step into the light. Sometimes we have to walk through darkness to realize we are light at our very core. Now Melissa is a light for others, helping them through their darkness. She holds the light with compassion and patience for all those who travel a journey like she did. There is always light in this world; sometimes we have to search to see it, but we are all light inside.

EXERCISE

Connecting to the Higher Self

Life can sometimes be overwhelming, especially when we encounter change or conflict. We may feel alone and isolated. But when we connect to the higher self, the spirit version of ourselves, we realize that we always have all the love and support we need. I use this exercise sometimes in client sessions, but you can do it anytime you need to feel love and support.

The higher self is the true essence of you—part of your soul. It's your total and complete version of yourself, free of projections, issues, imprints, and fears—the divine form of you. What exists on the earth plane is basically a small part of your total self that is engaging in physical life. The higher self oversees the human self; once engaged, the higher self provides deep guidance for navigating life on earth.

We can connect our human selves at any time to receive help from the higher self. But if we clear out our fears and projections and raise our vibrations, we can be closer to our higher selves on a regular basis. The higher self is in the vibration of unconditional love, so the more time we spend in that vibration, the closer we are to merging with our higher selves. This means choosing to look at experiences from a soul perspective rather than an ego-based one, realizing that all experiences are for our highest good. It also means engaging in kindness towards others and completely loving and accepting ourselves.

Until we reach the point where the human self and higher self merge and are vibrating at the rate of pure unconditional love, we have the ability to engage with our higher self through meditation. As we connect to the higher self, a sense of total peace and unconditional love envelops us. It is at this point that we become fully aware of how many things we need to clear from our human life. Connecting to the higher self helps us realize how and what we should be feeling all the time. When we connect we receive information about how we can improve our lives, if we just listen. It's time to live life as your soul chose before you incarnated. Connect with your higher self, be linked to the vibration of unconditional love, get on your soul path, and start living a life full of love!

What you will need for this exercise: your mind in a
relaxed state and a place to recline

* * * *

Close your eyes and breathe in deeply and release it. Do this a few times until you feel you're breathing comfortably in a relaxed state.

Place both hands over your heart chakra, in the center of your chest, and feel the energy vibrating there.

Next, envision a golden cord starting from your heart chakra and running up through the center of your body. See it going through your neck and your head and coming out the top of your head, through the crown chakra.

Picture the cord going from the top of your head and extending up into the sky until you can no longer see the end of it. Send loving energy from your heart chakra up the cord.

As you are sending loving energy up the cord, you feel something attach to the other end of the cord. Although you cannot see what is attached, you feel the loving energy it is sending down the cord to you.

Allow this warm, loving energy to fill your heart chakra. As it fills the chakra, then let it spill out and fill your entire body with the vibration of unconditional love. Allow this energy to flow in you!

As the cord moves closer to you, there is someone coming into view attached to the other end. It is your higher self, the perfect, radiant version of yourself that resides in the divine realm.

Now the higher self is in full view, and you can feel the vibration they carry. It is the vibration of unconditional love, and it is so overwhelming that you cannot contain it.

Using your mind, communicate telepathically with your higher self and ask what advice they can provide to guide you in this life. Spend a few moments communicating with your higher self. Make a mental note of everything communicated to you.

Now it is time for the higher self to return to the divine realm. See the cord attached to the higher self ascending back into the sky until you can no longer view the higher self.

Now detach the cord from your heart chakra and allow it to ascend to the sky. Watch as it becomes absorbed into the atmosphere.

Spend a few moments recounting the information your higher self shared with you.

Send thoughts of gratitude to your higher self for this experience. Know that you can connect to your higher self anytime you need to feel that love and support or guidance.

When you stand up, with your feet pressed against the ground, envision tree roots gently entangling around your feet, grounding you and holding you close to the earth.

• • • •

10

Understanding the Connections

I met Carolyn Miller in a seemingly roundabout way, but what appears coincidental to us is often an act of divine intervention; everything happens exactly as it should with regard to soul agreements. We encounter everyone we are supposed to meet and share the experiences needed for our development. I had donated a free healing session to a charitable organization. Carolyn's sister won the gift certificate and came for her session. She had an amazing experience and was able to connect with a few of her family members in spirit. Her older brother, Allen, whom she was very close with and held in high regard, stayed for over thirty minutes and shared pertinent information with her about the goings-on in her life. As a result, she referred Carolyn to me for a healing session, and what occurred was nothing short of miraculous. It opened my eyes to something beautiful and amazing, and I'm forever changed by the experience.

Other than knowing that her sister had referred her, I knew nothing of Carolyn. When the tall, thin middle-aged woman with light brown shoulder-length hair stepped through my office door the room immediately filled with the energy of kindness; she exuded it like her own personal brand of perfume. Carolyn took a seat in a chair across from me as her bright eyes conveyed the gentleness in her soul. We spoke for a few minutes about her sister and I talked about what to expect in the healing session, as I did with every new client. Then I led her to the table for our session. I pulled the white sheets and matching soft blanket up to her chest.

"I feel a little nervous…well, maybe not nervous—more like excited," she said and giggled innocently.

"Don't be nervous! It's going to be great," I commented. I said the opening prayer to center and shield the space and both of us. Then we began the session. I removed everything other than the highest vibration of love from her energetic field, and a gray energy filled with sadness lifted; then her vibration seemed lighter and I felt her physically relax.

She said that she suddenly felt peaceful. I told her that she was letting go of some old stuff.

"I'm sure I've got a lot of it," she said with a big smile.

"Everyone does from this life," I said to reassure her.

"Well, that's good to know," she said. Within a few seconds a tall brown-haired main in spirit stood toward the right of the table. He told me that he was her brother. I recognized him because we had met in her sister's session. I told Carolyn about her visitor.

"Allen!" she said affectionately as tears glistened in her eyes. He started joking with her and immediately the energy lightened. She laughed at the things he was saying. I knew by his energy that he could be a bit of a jokester. He teased his sister about being so serious all the time, but he said that she was laid back compared to her husband, George. Carolyn chuckled and agreed with him. He told me that she had left her house extra early that morning, giving herself an additional forty-five minutes of time in case she got lost or hit traffic. He said that she was a big planner and organized everything in her life. Carolyn concurred with everything he said.

The two enjoyed the joyful reunion, but then a young woman in spirit wearing a white nightgown appeared right next to Carolyn's face. She had straight long brown hair and stood silently next to her. I described the woman to Carolyn and said the woman told me she was thirty. Immediately, she knew the spirit.

"She's my daughter who passed. I had hoped she would be here," Carolyn said. The spirit came closer and said that she had left the earth as a baby, and Carolyn confirmed this by nodding her head. Carolyn explained that the baby had stopped moving and her heart had stopped beating at twenty-eight weeks, and Carolyn had had to deliver her as a stillborn. The experience had been incredibly traumatic for Carolyn, as she had been just twenty-four years old and the child had been the first for her and her husband.

At the time, Carolyn had been a nurse on a surgical floor of a hospital. She had struggled with the loss because there weren't any real resources to help her cope with her grief. She joined a support group and thought she would like to help other mothers with their grief. The support group leader encouraged her to heal her own grief before trying to help any other people. Carolyn worked through it, but the process was long, with very little support to assist her.

As she healed through the experience, she decided to switch from the surgical unit to the labor and delivery unit. Carolyn went through the professional nursing training to make the transition because she felt a burning desire help other mothers deal with and heal through the losses of their babies. After she completed her training, she began working with mothers in the labor and delivery unit; she's been there for the last thirty years.

In that time, Carolyn has helped implement changes in the hospital where she works. She moderates a support group for grieving mothers. The group, entitled Resolve Through Sharing, was a local chapter of a nationwide organization that helps mothers heal their grief by connecting and supporting each other. She also helped change hospital protocol so mothers have closure with their babies. Through these changes, mothers were afforded a chance to bond with their babies through the physical contact of holding them, bathing them, and saying goodbye in a gentle, loving way.

When Carolyn experienced the loss of her daughter thirty years earlier, none of those things were in place to help her or any other mothers handle their losses.

"The baby was taken away, and I never got a chance to say goodbye. Without any closure, you can't begin the healing process," she said.

Her daughter said that everything had happened as it should have for both of them. She explained that there was a soul agreement between the two of them. The agreement was that the baby's soul would leave before the birth, and as a result of that situation Carolyn would heal through the experiences and learn to help others heal. That is exactly what Carolyn did! She had a strong faith and she took the loss and used it as a vehicle to help others heal. If her daughter hadn't have passed that way, perhaps Carolyn never would have left the surgical unit and made the jump to labor and delivery. She might not have implemented those changes in the hospital procedures and helped all those mothers who encountered losses after her.

The daughter's soul needed a mother with strong faith to agree to such a contract. If Carolyn hadn't had that faith, the experience could have broken her, but it didn't. It changed the trajectory of her life in a beautiful way. As I was relaying the daughter's information to Carolyn, she was crying.

"I always knew God had a reason for it, and I believed in time I would find out what it was really about," she said tearfully. Just then the daughter stepped back and I couldn't even count the number of orbs that entered the healing space and circled around the bed. It looked like a ring of softball-sized pastel-colored bubbles three or four rings deep. I didn't really know what was happening, but the energy shifted to a feeling of overwhelming love. I couldn't contain the feeling of pure love, and it moved me so deeply that I began to cry. I explained to Carolyn what I saw. Although she couldn't see the soft orbs of light, she could feel their warm, loving energy. One of the orbs communicated telepathically and said that they were the souls of babies whom Carolyn had helped and they were there to thank her for helping them and their mothers. This information hit me right in the heart chakra. I felt so blessed to be part of such an incredible experience—all of these pure souls in the same place at the same time delivering a message of deep gratitude. Carolyn was overwhelmed by the message and the connection she had to all these other souls.

"Thank you for allowing me to help you and all of your mothers," she said aloud to all of them tearfully.

I had encountered the high vibrations of infants' souls in other sessions, but never so many in one session. The souls of infants and those not born full-term are purely divine energy because they have not had time to become tainted by the experiences on earth. It was such an incredible experience for both of us. After the session Carolyn and I sat in my office for an hour. We hugged, cried, and talked about the amazing session.

We struggle when our loved ones leave the earth. But unless they're suicidal deaths, with the specific intention to take one's own life, God has planned for all the passings. Once in a while we are given very special information about why these things happen, so we have a deeper understanding and can heal ourselves and the energy link between ourselves and our loved ones. Sessions like this one remind us all that life is a beautiful gift to be cherished, and we are always deeply connected to the souls of others.

EXERCISE

Accepting Experiences with Love for Our Highest Good

We have many experiences in our lives. Some of them affect us in positive ways and others may have negative affects. If the experiences have had major impacts on our lives, they may also be imprinted in the energetic field. Until we clear and heal those imprints, we may attract similar situations or people and patterns to us. All of these situations have purposes in our lives. Maybe they arose to help us clear karma, teach us lessons, or help us evolve. When we accept the fact that all situations are for our highest good, we can embrace things with open arms and love for all those involved. We can see clearly that there is a path set before us full of twists and turns, and once we travel it we will be changed in a wonderful, deeply loving way.

What you will need for this exercise: your mind in a relaxed state and a place to recline

• • • •

Lie flat, close your eyes, and place one hand over your heart chakra, in the center of your chest.

Place your other hand over your high heart chakra, located just a few inches above the heart chakra. It is equidistant between the heart chakra in the center of the chest and the throat chakra located in the center of the throat.

Now that you have one hand over the heart chakra and the other over the high heart chakra, breathe in deeply and release it slowly. Do this five times.

Feel the energy bouncing up from your heart chakra into your high heart chakra. Allow the energy to pulse there for a few minutes.

Next, envision your crown chakra, at the top of your head, opening and expanding. You may actually feel a little lightheaded as you do this. What you are actually feeling is your vibration shifting higher, and the lightheadedness is what it feels like when your energy is ungrounded.

See a shaft of golden light coming down from above you and entering your crown chakra. You may feel a bit of warmth and a little emotional as you allow this divine energy to move into your crown chakra.

As this energy fills your crown chakra, use your mind and thank the Divine for all the experiences in your life. Mention that you have a deep understanding and trust that even challenging times were meant for your highest good. You may also thank your spirit guides and higher self at this point for helping you navigate this life on earth.

Feel the energy from the crown chakra moving down into the high heart chakra. As it does this, you may sense an overwhelming vibration of love that brings you to tears. This chakra brings you into a deeper sense of love of one's self and others as well as of the Divine. Allow the energy from the crown chakra to balance the high heart chakra for a couple of minutes. As you feel the energy shift and balance in this area, use your mind to telepathically say, "I am connected to everyone and everything in my life in the deepest, most loving way."

Next, feel the energy shift from the high heart chakra down to the heart chakra, in the center of the chest. Allow the energy to shift and balance in this area and use your mind to telepathically say, "I am unconditionally loving of myself and all those around me."

Allow the energy to flow up and down between your crown and heart chakras. Feel yourself relaxing in the vibration of unconditional love. Know that all things happening in this life are for your highest good.

Place your hands by your sides and picture a red cord from your root chakra, at the base of your spine, flowing down through the ground and to the center of the earth.

See the cord connect to the earth's bright red core. Feel all your energy being pulled down from your crown chakra through your body and out your feet. Feel the earth's magnetic pull connecting deeply within you. When you are ready, see the cord disconnecting from your root chakra and being reabsorbed by the earth's molten core. Know that you are deeply grounded and centered.

. . . .

11

*Healing the Energy
in Your Home*

We want to clear and balance the energy in our homes regularly, just as we do for the energy of our energetic fields. Our homes contain energetic imprints of everything— the people and all the events that occur there. If we have had a stressful week, the energy may be very heavy. Depending on what happens in the home, the energy could be perceived as light or dark and positive or negative. This energy can be felt by the family members who live in the household, and it can also be perceived by those who visit us. If someone is upset, there could be grief and sadness there. If we have had disagreements with others, that energy can be sensed.

We should clear the energy in our homes energetically the same way we clean our homes physically. It is a good idea to space clear daily, but if you can't do it daily, you should at a minimum clear the energy in your home once a week. If you don't do this, the energy can feel chaotic, and it might be hard to relax in the home. Have you ever gone house hunting and walked into a totally empty home, knowing nothing about its owner, but you feel uneasy in the house? Perhaps you feel panic or anxiety or maybe you feel sad in a certain room. You are picking up on the home's energy and imprints clairsentiently. As noted earlier, clairsentience is the psychic sense that allows us to perceive energy through feeling. We all have this ability, and some of us are more in tune with it than others. Depending on your level of clairsentience, you can feel all imprints from others and what is energetically imprinted wherever you go. If you are highly clairsentient, you should be clearing the energy in your home once daily.

There are several methods we can use to clear the energy in our homes. In this section we will highlight physical methods, but we will also go over a couple of visualization methods. You may find that visualization methods are easier to complete on a regular basis because they are often less time consuming than physical methods. So you might want to use a visualization method daily and perform it at the end of each night. You may want to also include a physical method once a week, just as you physically clean your home. I encourage you to try all methods, both visual and physical, at least once, to see which methods suit your needs. Then you can create a space-clearing routine that works with your schedule and energy.

Physical Methods

Physical methods of space clearing are great because they tangibly demonstrate the energy being cleared and lifted in a space. Not all people can visualize easily. Some people like the process of doing something physical, so they can make sure the process is actually being completed. Physical methods of space clearing are a little more time consuming than visualization techniques, but they are very effective.

Smudging

Smudging is a Native American tradition used to clear energy. It involves allowing the smoke of a smoldering herb bundle such as white sage, cedar, or sweetgrass to permeate a space, and as it does it removes any unwanted energy in the process. In my first book, *Discovering the Medium Within*, there is a chapter called "Smudging the Garage." In it I discuss the first time I ever smudged my home. I had a spirit in my garage who was turning off the circuit breaker and opening the laundry room door to let me know she was out there and needed help crossing over. At the time I didn't know anything about smudging, but I had heard it was a method used to clear unwanted energy. I stopped at a New Age store and picked up a sage bundle with some verbal instructions about smudging from the store clerk.

The next morning, as I let the dog out in the yard before work, one of the large garage doors opened on its own. It was the side of the two-car garage that didn't have an electronic door opener. So I closed the door and locked it, but later when I got out to my car the door was open again. I smudged the garage that day for the first time ever. I walked around the room blowing the gray smoke in all the corners while instructing all stagnant and negative energy to leave the space. But after I smudged, the spirit opened the side garage door, and as I grabbed the handle and tried to pull it shut, a force jerked on the other side of the door, pulling it open, and I heard a woman's desperate plea for help because she had taken her own life and was stuck between worlds. The smudging technique did not clear the spirit because it was not stagnant or negative; it was a recent passing and her spirit was earthbound because it had been a suicide. But she did want to cross, and her guides led her to me. That was the first earthbound spirit I crossed over to the spirit world. In addition to learning how to help a spirit cross over that day, I learned from my guides that when I want to clear the space, I need to say something more general, like "remove everything other than the highest vibration of love." Since that day, I smudge my home weekly, and if something challenging happens, like an argument or an emotionally distressing event, I smudge immediately.

EXERCISE

Smudging Your Home

Before we get into the exercise of smudging, I just want to cover a few basics you need to know when using this method of space clearing. First, when you light the herb bundle, ignite a few sprigs on one end, then blow it out or the bundle will quickly turn into a fiery torch. Blow out the flame and let the lit sprigs smolder into a thin film of smoke. Now the bundle is ready to smudge. Place a plate, bowl, or shell under the bundle to catch any falling embers as you walk through the house. Leave an open window in each room as an exit point for the unwanted energy being cleared. In addition, close any toilet lids and empty any standing open water containers, such as water bowls for pets, otherwise the residual energy will be deposited into the standing water.

When smudging a house, begin in one room and make your way through all the rooms on the lowest level. If you have a second level, you would proceed up there and follow the same process of moving from one room to the next. It is also a good idea to smudge the perimeter of your home, as well as any attached garage space. Once you are done smudging, you will need to make sure the bundle is fully extinguished. Some people do this by immersing the lit end in water or sand.

> *What you will need for this exercise:* a smudge bundle, matches or a lighter, and a plate, bowl, or shell to catch any loose embers
>
> • • • •
>
> Light the smudge stick and blow out the flame so it is smoldering. After doing this, place the plate, bowl, or shell under the smudge stick.
>
> Walk into the first room and open a window. Also open any closet or pantry doors in the room. Next, say, "I clear and release anything other than the highest vibration of love. This house is filled with love, light, and tranquility." Repeat this as you walk through the room. Be sure to blow the thin smoke in all corners of the room.
>
> Once you complete smudging one room, move into the next one and open a window and any

closets. Repeat the affirmation while blowing the smoke in all corners of the room.

Do this for every room in the first level of the house and repeat the process in any additional levels.

When you are through smudging all rooms in all levels of your home and any additional areas such as a garage or the home's perimeter, you can extinguish the smoldering smudge stick. Do this by dipping the smoldering end in a bowl of water or sand. Make sure all the smoldering embers are completely extinguished before putting the smudge stick away.

* * * *

WATER

Another method used to clear the space involves bowls or cups of water. This physical method is good for someone who will change the water once a week. With this method, a small bowl or cup of water is placed in each room of the house. This gives the unwanted energy a place to be deposited. The cups are set in each room and the water is replaced once a week. This is a method I used when Brayden was a little baby, but it proved to be problematic as he became a toddler. I had a small cup of water in each room of the house. There was a big bowl in the kitchen and a big one in the dining room. One day when I was putting Brayden's clean laundry away in his bureau, I saw him in the upstairs hallway—he was drinking the little cup of water I had set out on the ledge to catch the residual energy.

"Oh, no, no," I said as I walked toward him.

He removed the cup from his lips and said, "I drink, Mama," then he beamed a smile of accomplishment across his little face.

"Sweetie, those are not for drinking," I began to explain, and then I realized that at three he wouldn't understand why I had the cup of water there. Plus, it was a perfect size for his little hands, so he most likely thought it was there for him to drink regularly. That was the last day I used the water cups to balance and clear the energy in our home. I collected all of them one by one, dumped the water in the toilet, and thought about a new method of clearing.

There are some rudimentary points I want to cover about using water bowls and cups to balance the energy in your home. As I mentioned earlier, when we smudge we close toilet lids and empty any open containers of water so that residual energy does not get deposited there. In this method of space clearing we leave a bowl or cup of water in each room. In doing so, we give the energy and imprints a place to be deposited. Then, when needed, we dispose of the water and replace it with new water. Some people do this once a week and others may do it once a month. It depends on how long it takes for the energy to collect in the cup or bowl.

A good test of this method is to place a clear glass of water on a table in a room where an argument or stressful situation has taken place. When you allow the water to sit out overnight, you will notice that the following morning the glass has little bubbles lined along the sides. This is the residual energy that has been trapped in the water. Dump this water in the toilet or down the drain. Do not drink it or feed it to plants or animals. In addition to the other methods of space clearing that I employ in my office, I keep a big clear glass bowl of water on the mantle and I change it weekly.

If you notice a number of bubbles being retained in the water, you will want to dump the water immediately. Some rooms may require a bigger bowl. The kitchen and den might be places where there are lots of interaction in contrast to the bedrooms, where you might only spend time sleeping. Initially, when you set out the bowls, you will want to check them daily for bubbles. You may find one area of your home that retains more energy than others. You might have to replace the water in this area a couple of times a week at first.

EXERCISE

Water Collection Method

What you will need for this exercise: cups (or bowls) and water

. . . .

Fill the cups with water. You will need one cup for each room.

Place one cup on a table, counter, or dresser in each room.

Check the cups daily for bubbles.

If there aren't bubbles, you will only need to change the water once a week.

If you find the water is retaining bubbles, you will need to change the water immediately.

Make a mental note of any cups in rooms that accumulate bubbles more quickly than other spaces. These areas will need to be monitored more closely and the water changed more frequently.

To change the water, collect each cup from every room and dispose of the water in either the sink or the toilet.

Then you will refill the cups with fresh water and place them in each room again. Do this weekly.

* * * *

SALT

By its very nature, salt has cleaning and healing properties. Like water, it is a fundamental element of the earth. It can be used to clean surfaces and the air. In my office I have a bunch of salt lamps that provide lighting during my evening client sessions. The lamps emit a cleansing vibration. Many of my clients use the lamps as night lights or night stand lamps in the bedrooms of their homes. As the lamps heat up, they disperse the salt gently in the air. They give rooms very soothing effects. Salt can be a deeply healing element for our bodies. It is a necessary component for us to establish internal homeostasis, and it heals surface wounds. If you have a cut or an abrasion, swimming in the ocean water cleanses and helps these injuries heal quickly.

I incorporated the salt method after I found Brayden drinking the water in the energy collection cup in the upstairs hallway. We live close to the ocean and even closer to the bay, so we are use to smelling salt in the air regularly. First, I incorporated salt in the bedrooms. I decided to buy a salt lamp for Brayden's room as a nightlight. When I would go to check in on him at night, the gentle orange hue gave off such a peaceful vibration, so I chose to buy one for each of the bedrooms. The salt lamps were on each night, and the energy was very balanced and gentle. I liked the way it made the rooms feel, so I decided to include salt in each room of the house downstairs too.

I didn't think the salt lamps would be a fit for the downstairs décor, so I bought salt candle holders. I purchased large square white ones that held a thick pillar candle. I placed four of them in the room, each one in a different corner on either a shelf or an end table. Whenever I burn the candles, the holders heat up and emit salt into the air, but even without the candles lit, the salt disperses in the room from the humidity. I bought smaller salt candle holders for the kitchen, dining room, and living room. I placed them in the corners of the rooms and let them emit the salt in the air as needed. Salt is such a basic component in balancing the energy in the home, yet it makes a noticeable difference in the home's vibration.

There are some basic points to review when incorporating salt in your home's energy balancing. The point of including salt in the home is to add another layer of energy cleansing. The main goal is to have a component of salt in each room of the home. One important note: salt may be toxic to certain animals, so if you are using this exercise, you will want to place the salt up high and out of reach of pets and perhaps young children. The salt components can be salt lamps, salt candle holders, salt blocks, or a small bowl of salt (enough to hold a tablespoon of loose salt crystals). The salt will literally draw out the impurities (if any) in the room. It will also evaporate a bit in the air, depending on the humidity and temperature. Care must be taken with the salt lamps, candle holders, and blocks. They will liquefy and drip if exposed to excessive moisture and heat. Avoid putting them in direct sunlight. When they melt, they can stain wood or affect the finish on furniture. Be sure to place a small plate under any salt component to prevent it from liquefying and spilling onto your furniture.

Salt Method

What you will need for this exercise: components of
   salt (such as salt lamps, salt blocks, salt candle
   holders, or salt in small bowls) to be placed in
   each room of the house

• • • •

Decide which component will go in each room.
You may want to place a larger salt piece in a room
where you spend a lot of time, like a den or kitchen,
and you may want something smaller in a room
with less activity.

Place one element of salt in each room.

Leave the salt in place for three days. After that
time, check each room and see if the salt is intact
or if it needs to be replaced. You may find that you
need to shift things around a bit as far as which
components belong in which room.

If you are using salt in small bowls, you should
replace the salt once a week. Like the water exercise, dispose of unwanted salt in the toilet or down
a drain. Please be aware that salt in large quantities
will be corrosive to metal drainage pipes.

After about two weeks, you should have all the
salt components in the right places of your home.
Then you will just need to monitor and replace the
components as needed.

• • • •

CREATING CRYSTAL GRIDS

My favorite method of energy balancing and clearing in my home is setting a crystal grid. I incorporated this method right after I opened my first office and began working as a healing medium. Although I would psychically shield before a session and clear and cut cords when ending sessions, I was still attracting energy after the session and sometimes bringing it home.

Sometimes at night we would have spirit activity in the home. I remember one night I woke to a crashing noise downstairs. Both dogs growled and remarkably both Brayden and Briella slept right through it. I looked at the clock in my bedroom and it beamed 2:22 in bright red letters. *Perfect! This is exactly what I want to be doing at 2:00 a.m.*, I thought.

I walked downstairs and into the kitchen. I turned the light on and looked around but found nothing. I moved into the den and found everything intact. Then I made my way into the dining room. There on the wooden floor was a large picture frame that had been hanging on the wall. The glass had not broken and it was situated in a weird position that was unnatural considering where it had fallen from. The picture was faceup, as if someone had taken it off the wall and thrown it down. It should have fallen with the picture facing against the floor and the back of the frame facing up. It was clearly a strange situation. I picked it up and decided to take care of it later that morning, after I had a chance to gain more sleep. When I went up to bed I asked my guides for advice on how to minimize the energy coming into the home. Even though I clear the house each night, the kids were both picking up energy, plus sometimes I would fall asleep while clearing the energy in the home.

One guide said that I should consider putting a crystal grid in the downstairs and one in the upstairs, as well. I took out my notepad and pen that I keep next to my bed for notes from my guides. My guide gave me the specifics of why and how to set up a crystal grid. The next day I bought the clear quartz points, set them in salt to remove any mining residue, and then I set up the downstairs grid. I situated the grid downstairs because I wanted to assess if the energy actually felt differently, but it was immediate. It felt peaceful and balanced. The next day I set one in the upstairs as well. The energy felt the same as downstairs—peaceful. I think a small crystal grid is a fundamental component for every home.

Crystal grids can balance, shield, and cleanse the energy in any home or office space. When we set the crystals out in a pattern in any space, the points emit a beam of energy that is projected into the space. The beams of energy can go through walls and all physical objects. Multiple crystals create multiple beams. When we arrange them they form an energetic grid that can cleanse, balance, and shield the space. There are several different types of grids one can create, depending on the energetic effect desired. The grid exercise in this section is one designed to create balance and clear the energy in a space.

When we speak of balancing the energy in a space, we want its inhabitants and those people who visit the space to feel that the energy is peaceful and comfortable. We also want to use the crystals to cleanse the energy in the space of any lower vibrational imprints. As noted earlier, whatever happens in your home gets imprinted energetically in each room. The crystal grid transmutes that energy so it doesn't remain in the home. If someone has depression and spends a lot of time in a bedroom, the energy in that room will feel sad and heavy. It may even feel to some people like they are totally stifled and can't breathe in that room. Once the crystals are in place, people will feel a sense of peace. The energy will be cleared and lighter.

For the overall crystal grid in a home, I use clear quartz for a couple of reasons. It's the highest vibrational frequency of any crystal on earth at this point and it is self-cleansing, so you do not need to remove the crystals and soak them in salt water or sunlight every week. Because it is self-cleansing, it is also energetically cleansing the environment continuously. So, basically, you set the crystals in place, and the clear quartz does everything else.

For gridding spaces, we generally use one- to two-inch clear quartz points. They can be double or single terminated. Double terminated means there is a point at each end, and single terminated means there is one point and the other end of the crystal is flat. The crystals do not need to be large because the energy they emit is strong. If you hold a piece of the quartz in your hand, you can feel the vibration's strength.

If your home is square or rectangular in shape, you will place at minimum one crystal in each corner of your home. For example, if you have a living room in the right front corner of your house and a dining room in the left front corner of your home, you will place one crystal in the far corner of each room. You would do the same for the back corners of your home. So for a square one-level home, the grid will consist of four quartz points set in each corner of the home. If your home is more than one level, you will want to have a grid on each level. If your home is non-rectangular, you can add additional crystals to balance the grid. If the crystal has one point, position the point outward, with the flat end facing the wall. If the crystal has two points, or is double terminated, just place the crystal in the corner; it does not matter which point is facing outward.

As you create a grid in the lower level of a home, you will place one clear quartz point in each of the four corners of the home. These can be positioned in the corners on the floor, but if you have concerns about children or animals being injured by them or perhaps ingesting them, you can place them up higher on shelving. Once the crystals are in place, envision them connecting energetically, each one emitting a laser of energy outward from its point. Each point's laser of energy contributes to the grid. Energy is emitted from the point as well as out of the side of each crystal. Each crystal is releasing a vibrational laser from its point and connecting to the crystal positioned diagonally from it. Thus the space is being balanced, protected, and cleansed completely, not only on the perimeter but also through all the rooms of the first level.

BEDROOM GRIDS

Sometimes it is helpful to create additional grids in each bedroom. You can select the right crystal based on the individual person's overall vibration. I have a rose quartz grid on the floor in my daughter's room. She is a deeply compassionate child, so I wanted her room to feel loving and supportive for her. I did not use rose quartz points for her grid. I used rose quartz clusters. There is one cluster of rose quartz in each corner of her room.

For Brayden I have two grids. He has a rose quartz grid on the ceiling. I have situated a two-inch rose quartz pyramid in each corner of his room. The crystals are set on a shelf that runs below the crown molding around his entire room. On his floor I have a grid of blue lace agate, which is peaceful and calming, although I will need to raise this grid a bit. I have a three-inch tumbled piece of blue lace agate in each corner of the room.

Brayden has a litter-trained dwarf bunny named Hoppy that has an open cage in his room. She sleeps, eats, and goes to the bathroom in her litter pan in the cage, but she runs around the room and hangs out all day. We basically have an "open cage" policy for her. We keep all wires off the floor, and she enjoys being free in a safe environment. We acquired Hoppy by accident. My parents found her while kayaking along the river one day. She was sitting along the riverside. They stopped and picked her up because it was clear that the little white rabbit was domesticated. My parents weren't sure if she had gotten out of someone's yard or if someone had dropped her off in the woods, but they were afraid that she would not survive on her own. So they scooped her up and brought her to my house. They knew we had experience with house rabbits from November, and as soon as Brayden saw the soft white bunny, he wanted to keep her.

When I first set the blue lace agate grid out, I went in Brayden's room the next day to put his laundry on his dresser. I noticed one of the pieces of agate was missing. Then I checked the other three corners, and they were all missing. I looked all over the room and couldn't find them. Then Hoppy, who was reclining on his rug in the center of the room, rose and hopped into her cage. She had been sitting on all four pieces of the smooth agate—apparently she liked the vibration because she pulled all four pieces from the corners and set them in the center of the rug and had nestled herself on top of the pieces. I set the pieces out in the corners the next morning, and later that day I found her sitting on top of them in the center of the room again, so I think she needs her own piece of blue lace agate and Brayden's floor grid has to be moved higher to his shelving.

Although I use clear quartz for the overall grid for a home or office space, the vibration might be too strong for a bedroom. I have clear quartz in my bedroom, and the grid is set along the crown molding that runs along the ceiling. My energy is always strong. Sometimes my clients say they feel me vibrating when I hug them after a session. So for me, clear quartz is a good vibrational fit for the energy in my bedroom. But the energy is too strong for both my children to have in their rooms. If the vibration is not a fit, the person might feel wired at bedtime instead of feeling peaceful and relaxed. Choose crystals that are a vibrational fit for each person. When we go into our bedrooms, we want to feel calm.

Selenite is a great crystal to add to a bedroom grid because the vibration is gentle and peaceful. In my home I have long selenite pieces in all the bedrooms and the den. Once your grids are in place, allow them to set for a few days so you can get a feel for the energy. If you need to make an adjustment, you will feel it.

EXERCISE

Crystal Grids

This exercise can be used to grid a home or office space. Clear quartz works great for offices. I have a crystal grid on the floor in my office and along the ceiling. Since one side of my office comes up against a couple of doors that lead to other office spaces, I have separate grids at the bottoms and tops of all doors, as well. This keeps the energy from my space contained in my office and the energy of other offices in their spaces. I recommend office grids for anyone doing any type of therapeutic work or anyone who just finds the workplace energy overwhelming.

> *What you will need for this exercise:* one- to two-inch clear quartz points (single or double terminated)

> • • • •

> Set your clear quartz points in a bowl of salt water overnight. Although they are self-cleansing, it is important to remove any elemental dust they might contain from the mining process.

> Decide if it is safe to place the grid on your floor or higher up if you have animals and children.

> Place one crystal in each corner of your home. Be sure to face the point outward and the flat end toward the wall if you are using single terminated points.

> Add additional points if needed to balance the space.

> Place a grid in the same pattern upstairs and on any other levels of your home if you have more than one level.

> Allow the grid or grids to set in place for a few days, then check the energy in the house by walking through each room. Decide if you need additional crystals or if the space feels balanced.

Good luck with your grids, and may the energy in your home always be peaceful, balanced, and full of light.

• • • •

Grounding the Wireless Frequencies in Our Homes

For most of us, our homes are filled with technology devices wirelessly transmitting information. We have wireless routers for our internet, wireless phones, wireless cable devices for television signals, and some of our security systems run wirelessly. These devices support our expedient lifestyles and eliminate the need for cables and physical wires running everywhere. But all the wireless transmissions can affect the energy in our homes and ultimately affect us in a physical way. Too much of this energy in the home can make us feel amped up, making it hard to relax. There are a couple of ways we can balance the wireless energy running through our homes.

All wireless transmission devices should be removed from bedrooms. These rooms are places of peace and relaxation. Wireless devices will disrupt the peaceful energy in these rooms. Wherever there is a wireless router, you should put a large grounding stone right next to it. This will ground the energy being emitted from the device and block it from affecting the energy in the space. There are several types of grounding stones available. I like black obsidian because it is a fit for my energy. Certain stones are not a fit for me, such as tiger's-eye, which shatters if I wear it in jewelry. You may want to visit a metaphysical store and see which grounding stone fits your vibration. When a stone is a fit for your vibration, it feels gentle and calming when you hold it in your hand. Grounding stones are usually dark in color, like black, gray, or brown, and have a heavy sensation when you hold them in your palm. This is because the energy of the stone is in line with the earth's strong magnetic current. As a result, the stone draws your energy downward, deeply connecting you to the earth.

Some types of grounding stones include black obsidian, tiger's-eye, hematite, smokey quartz, onyx, and black tourmaline. I usually buy mine online, but sometimes I just find them in odd shops or maybe they find me. For example, I picked up the big piece of obsidian that grounds our internet router in a toy store. You should have a grounding stone next to each wireless device in the home. Technology is great and improves our lives, but we need to keep the energy of it balanced in our homes.

Visualization Methods

If you are familiar with my first book, *Discovering the Medium Within,* you might recall that I highlighted some visualization techniques for space clearing in the back of the book. I am a huge fan of visualization techniques because if you are a visual person, they are easy to complete and require very little time. The methods I highlight in the section require only the use of your mind and can be completed in less than three minutes. For this reason you might want to add a visualization method to your daily space-clearing routine. In my home I use a visualization technique every night.

I used to employ a tunneling white light exercise to clear the house every night, but as our vibrations increased, so did the energy in the home. As we raised our frequencies, we attracted different energy. I noticed this shift and asked my guides if I should be doing anything else to make sure the home was clear each night, so everyone could enjoy a restful slumber. My guide directed me to using the rainbow light technique because it incorporated the full spectrum of light. The first night that I used it the energy felt different. Instead of just feeling peaceful and clear, it felt warm, loving, and gently vibrant. It is definitely a different vibration. I also feel a bit of joy in it. It actually reminds me of Briella's overall vibration. Since that first evening, I use it each night because it is the perfect way to clear the energy in my home.

EXERCISE

Rainbow Light Space Clearing

When we engage this exercise we are including the full spectrum of light to enter our home and cast that energy throughout. In doing so, it clears and transmutes all imprints as well as raises the home's vibration. This exercise is not only visually stimulating but also relays a deep sense of tranquility as you work with it. I love it and use it regularly in my own home at night to clear the energy from the day.

What you will need for this exercise: your focused mind

• • • •

Close your eyes and sense the collective vibration of your home's energy.

Tilt your head back toward the sky. Visualize in your mind a vibrantly colored rainbow. As you take in this brightly colored rainbow, it seems like it is moving toward your home. You realize it is, and one end of the rainbow is descending right over your home.

One by one, the brilliant colors enter your roof and beam down to where you are standing. First you see warm red, then gentle orange, next sunny yellow, then lush green, cooling blue, deep indigo, and vibrant violet.

As they enter the space, they swirl around and bathe the room in colorful light. It feels warm and peaceful, and the room glows in the rainbow's hues.

See the bright colors dispersed throughout the room and sense the energy becoming lighter. Once the energy is cleared in one room, the colors move on to the next one.

The colorful rainbow goes through each room of the house, painting it in bright hues and warming it from the inside out.

As it completes this process in the last room of the house, you see the colors lifting and going back toward the ceiling, taking with them all the unwanted energy and imprints they collected in their coloring process.

The colors rise through the roof and back up to the sky, leaving behind only warm, gentle, peaceful energy.

You see the rainbow moving away from your home and ascending higher and higher until it is just a brief colorful outline in the sky.

Once the rainbow completely disappears, walk through each room in your home. You can discern the difference in the home's energy. It is calm and relaxing. Each room feels tranquil.

· · · ·

Managing the energy in our homes is just as important as managing our energetic fields. Our homes are an extension of us. We spend a lot of time there, and we want our homes to be places of peace—respite from the chaos of everyday life. I hope you can find at least one physical space-clearing method or a combination of a couple that resonate with you. I also hope that you either use the rainbow visualization exercise for space clearing or one of the visualization exercises from my first book each day to clear the energy in your home. Once you get used to the exercise, it will become second nature and you will do it automatically.

May your home be a peaceful place filled with the vibration of unconditional love.

Anysia

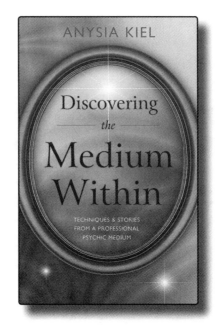

To order, call 1-877-NEW-WRLD
or visit llewellyn.com

Prices subject to change without notice

Discovering the Medium Within

Techniques & Stories from a
Professional Psychic Medium

Anysia Kiel

Anysia Kiel invites us to witness the wondrous, dramatic, and truly beautiful moments that have shaped her life as a psychic medium. Her powerful life story—communicating with deceased family members and friends to bring comfort, healing, and peace to the living—will inspire you to embark on your own journey of psychic awakening.

Seeing spirits everywhere—in her bedroom at night, on buses and streets, and in graveyards—was terrifying for young Anysia. Then one day her own grandmother in spirit reached out to her, giving Anysia the strength and courage to begin a journey of self discovery that forever changed her life. Discover how she learns, with help from her spirit guides, how to develop and control her profound gift for spirit communication and energy healing. Her touching story, filled with miraculous spiritual encounters, concludes with Anysia's personal techniques for psychic development to help you reunite with your own loved ones in spirit.

978-0-7387-3667-9

$5^3/_{16}$ x 8

240 pp.

To Write to the Author

If you wish to contact the author or would like more information about this book, please write to the author in care of Llewellyn Worldwide and we will forward your request. Both the author and the publisher appreciate hearing from you and learning of your enjoyment of this book and how it has helped you. Llewellyn Worldwide cannot guarantee that every letter written to the author can be answered, but all will be forwarded.

Please write to:

Anysia Marcell Kiel
^{c}/o Llewellyn Worldwide
2143 Wooddale Drive
Woodbury, MN 55125-2989

Please enclose a self-addressed stamped envelope for reply
or $1.00 to cover costs. If outside the USA, enclose
an international postal reply coupon.

Many of Llewellyn's authors have websites with additional information and resources. For more information, please visit our website:

LLEWELLYN.COM